FINANCIAL BLACK HOLES February 2019

HOW TO PLUG FINANCIAL BLACK HOLES

This book has been written with the intention of
encouraging readers to
Consider carrying out a process review of their
management system to
ascertain if it is efficient, effective and can be justified.

This would allow the organization to obtain information to
enable them to modify their system using objective and
factual evidence to reduce
CHRONIC WASTE

This could prevent cash flow hemorrhaging into the
financial Black Hole

Care has to be taken to ensure that procedures and
other documents being used do not overrule
COMMON SENSE

DAVID JOHN SEEAR

FINANCIAL BLACK HOLES   February 2019

Published by New Generation Publishing in 2019

Copyright © PDQ Management Services 2019

First edition of "How to plug Financial Black Holes"

Note: - This first edition was developed after the author acted as a principle speaker at the 26th ISO 9000 World Conference in Las Vegas in April 2018. The presentation was called "Professional Process Auditing and Reviews". It had been agreed with the conference organizers that following the presentation it would be acceptable to ask delegates if they would like to provide feedback. Following that presentation feedback was received from 20% of the delegates. This book is in the response to their concerns.
This is the fifth book in a series of books around management and improvement

The previous books: -
ISO 9001:2015 Into the Future ISBN: 978-1-5049-9428-6 (sc)
ISO 9001 Back to the future ISBN 978-1-4969-9807-1 (sc)
ISO 9001- 2012 Audit Trail ISBN 978-1-4772-3489-1 (sc)
ISO 9000:2012 Family of Standards ISBN 978-1-4772-2640-7 (sc)

All the above books are available as ebooks
ISO 9001:2015 Into the Future ISBN 978-1-5049-9429-3 (e)
ISO 9001 Back to the future ISBN 978-1-4969-9809-5 (e)
ISO 9001- 2012 Audit Trail ISBN 978-0-9565100-0-6 (e)
ISO 9000:2012 Family of Standards ISBN 978-1-4771-2640-4 (e)

The previous books published by Author House are intended for all types of organization both manufacturing and service industries as well as Accreditation, Certification Bodies and their auditors. The previous book "ISO 9001 2015 Into the Future" highlight the importance of reading all of the standard and not just the requirement sections. This is because in many cases the failure to read the introduction and Annex A and B of ISO 9001:2015 has led to the requirement clauses being used out of context.

This new book is generic and suitable for any organization where improvement is considered beneficial. It highlights the growing number of organisations that live with "Chronic Waste" and have little or no drive to improve. The book identifies the importance of gathering information in order to manage the improvement process in an effective manner.

The guidance notes, drawings, proposals may not be used or copied without approval @ 2019 David John Seear. All rights reserved.

No part of this book may be reproduced, stored in a retrieval system, or transmitted by any means without the written permission of the author.

Many of the images has been produced by the author and www.dabagency.co.uk for illustrative purposes

ISBN: 978-1-78955-417-5
www.newgeneration-publishing.com

 **New Generation** Publishing

 FINANCIAL BLACK HOLES   February 2019

INDEX

INDEX 1

1.0 - INTRODUCTION 3

2.0 - CHRONIC WASTE 5

3.0 - IMPORTANT VOCABULARY AND DEFINITIONS 10

4.0 - SUMMARY WHERE INEFFECTIVE ACTIVITIES ARE NOT RECOGNISED 15

5.0 - SUMMARY WHERE INEFFECTIVE ACTIVITY HAS BEEN RECOGNISED 28

6.0 - SUMMARY OF EXAMPLES GIVEN 33

7.0 - HOW TO IMPROVE 35

8.0 - AUDITING 39

9.0 - LEADERSHIP 53

10.0 - IMPROVEMENT REGARDING THE EXAMPLES 62

11.0 - GENERAL IMPROVEMENT 71

12.0 - HOW TO LOOK FOR OPPORTUNITIES TO IMPROVE? 80

13.0 - TRADITIONAL DOCUMENTED SYSTEM STRUCTURE 91

14.0 - CONCLUSION, CONCERN AND OPPORTUNITIES 96

ATTACHMENT A: AQI 26th Annual World Conference 100

ATTACHMENT B: David Rutley MP Meeting Friday 30th June 2017 .. 103

ATTACHMENT C: Conscious Competence Model 107

ATTACHMENT D: ISO 9001 Auditing Practicer Group Audit Trail 109

ATTACHMENT E: Problem Sheet 113

ATTACHMENT F: Audit Plan 114

ATTACHMENT G: Back to Basics guidance documents 120

ABOUT THE AUTHOR 150

PROGRESSION OF BOOKS 152

Note: - Not all definitions in this book are recognised by other professionals

FINANCIAL BLACK HOLES

February 2019

 FINANCIAL BLACK HOLES   February 2019

1.0 - INTRODUCTION

All the views in this book are the author's and are an attempt to help organisations both large and small to accept that not all management systems are effective. The book asks personnel involved in carrying out any type of assessment to judge if what is being done is effective, provides information and can be justified?

This book has been developed to expand on the presentation carried out by David John Seear at the American Quality Institutes (AQI) 3 day 26th ISO 9001World Conference in Las Vegas in April 2018. All of the delegates who took the time to respond and provide feedback on the presentation titled "Professional Process Audit and Reviews" recognised that there was a need to improve what takes place however they were concerned how it could be achieved.
(See Att A)

This book is intended to provide a simple approach to how improvement can be managed by using a sample of the concerns presented at the World Conference to illustrate where activities are not effective. The next step in the process is to obtain realistic information on how improvement could be implemented. The book covers the need to investigate any areas where complaints, non-conformities or other failures cause financial loss in terms of time, credibility or efficiency. The intention is to reduce waste by plugging financial loss.

It is important that readers recognise that each chapter of the book is intended to be standalone. As such there is some repetition for clarity

The book also covers effective assessment of processes and the importance of meaningful management reviews. It requires Leadership to obtain information and identify the "Root Cause" of any problem in order to prevent it happening again. This would then reduce "Chronic Waste" and achieve a consistent acceptable outcome.

The first step is to obtain information.

The book is intended to assist organisations in the private sector and the public sector to identify opportunities to improve. Reducing losses where

 FINANCIAL BLACK HOLES February 2019

financial income is hemorrhaging down "Black Holes" provides an ongoing financial saving.

The book identifies some examples that are the cause of "Chronic Waste". This is where organisations carry out ineffective audits and/or management reviews or fail to investigate complaints and other opportunities to improve in an effective manner. In too many cases what takes place does not identify the root cause of the problem or identify where processes are effective and ineffective so management can take action to prevent the problem recurring.

The book highlights how, in many cases, the activities undertaken by so called professionals are not consistent and in some instances just assess an organizations systems regardless of how effective those systems are. This has led to the term: -

"WITHOUT REASONABLE CARE AND SKILL"

As an ex naval officer plugging any leaks in any area is a desirable activity

FINANCIAL BLACK HOLES   February 2019

2.0 - CHRONIC WASTE

"Chronic Waste" was recognised by the Quality Guru J M Juran many decades ago. His method of dealing with this, through projects, was developed and illustrated in his quality improvement training material copyrighted in his workbook published in 1981.

It is not the intention within this book to do any more than use the term Chronic Waste to highlight that unless an organisation recognises that what is being done is ineffective then they will continue to waste finances and resources.

So what is **Chronic Waste?** The term **Chronic** means: - Lasting for a long time.

This is mainly associated with **illness** or a **problem** and within this book it is dealing with a **problem.** The term waste has various meanings and when dealing with a problem it means: -
Waste (Noun) doing something in a manner that is ineffective. (Wasteful)

So **"Chronic Waste"** when it relates to a problem means: -

CONTINUING TO CARRY OUT AN ACTIVITY IN AN INEFFECTIVE MANNER

<u>STAGES OF CHRONIC WASTE</u>

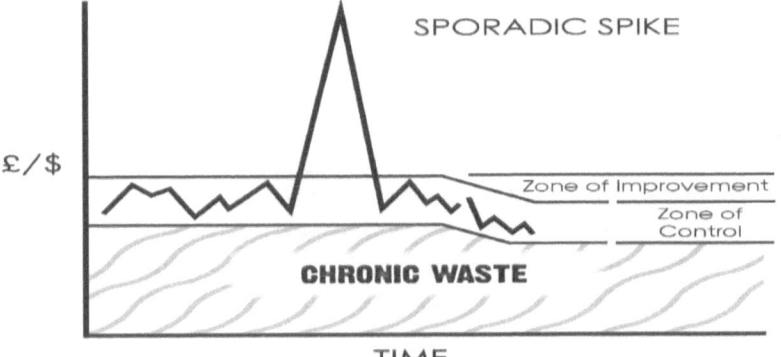

FINANCIAL BLACK HOLES   February 2019

This drawing illustrates the various stages of "Chronic Waste". On the left is the "Static Zone of Control" where "Chronic Waste" is accepted. The "Sporadic Spike" is where a large costly incident consumes a lot of the organisation cash flow just to bring it back to the "Zone of Control". On the right is what happens when any non-conforming incident is investigated to identify the "Root Cause" of the problem. The organisation then carries out "Corrective Action" that eliminates the cause and prevents it happening again. This reduces "Chronic Waste".

The intention within this book is to use the presentation carried out in the USA entitled **"Professional process Auditing and Reviews"** to illustrate what is currently taking place. This presentation consisted of some examples where what took place was ineffective. (See Section 4 Summary where ineffective activity is not recognised)

STATIC CHRONIC WASTE

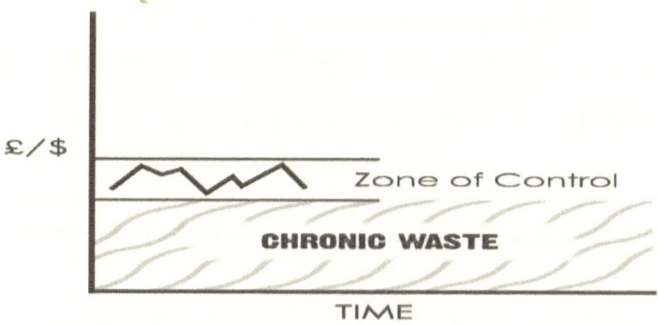

The above diagram illustrates how organisations can quite happily live within their "zone of control" yet allow "chronic waste" to be ignored. This shows where no action is taken to reduce it because everyone accepts that this level of waste is normal. The area below the Zone Of Control, marked as Chronic Waste, illustrates that no effort is made to reduce this loss as it remains the same.

Many organisations accept a "zone of control" that can leave Chronic Waste at anything from 5% to 15% of turnover as they are only carrying out correction. This approach fails to investigate the "root cause" of the problem. This chronic waste can even be as much as 20% in some organisations.

6

FINANCIAL BLACK HOLES   February 2019

From experience a lot of individuals who have been on training courses run by the author have indicated that their organisation suffers from complaints or where activities have taken place that do not meet customer requirements. This leads to work having to be redone and where, on occasion, payments have to be made to the customer to compensate them. This approach often only applies a "Correction". In other words making things right. This is because everyone has become so used to problems that there is no interest in improving what takes place.

The only time some organisations try to deal with a problem is when it becomes a "Sporadic Spike". A sporadic spike is where the cost of dealing with the problem is excessive. An example of this is the Grenfell Tower Fire where, due to the horror of the fire and the public outcry, it could not be ignored. This is where too many organisations spend more time and money defending what they have done rather than investigating the "Root Cause" of the problem. All evidence indicated that the problem occurred due to the manner in which the Grenfell Tower refurbishment was carried out. A significant priority seems to have been the price of the refurbishment. The Government Enquiry into the Grenfell Tower Fire was given a much broader scope. Section 4C of this book gives a short summary that covers examples of how the action taken has failed to concentrate on the principle root cause of the problem.

<u>SPORADIC SPIKE</u>

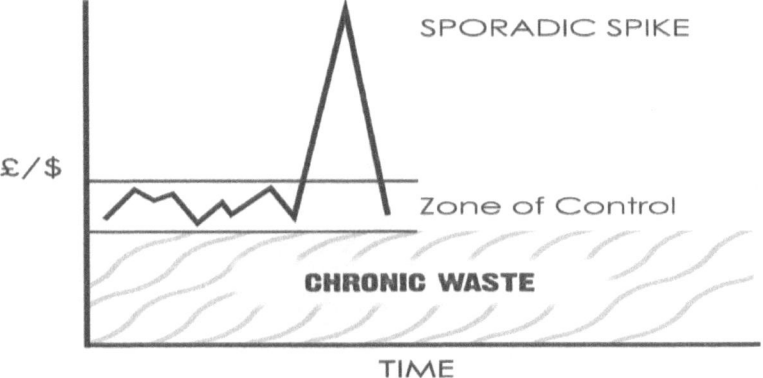

Just bringing the problems back to the "Zone of Control" quite often fails to achieve improvement because there is no attempt to carry out "Corrective Action".

FINANCIAL BLACK HOLES   February 2019

Corrective Action is defined as: -
Action to eliminate the cause of a nonconformity to prevent recurrence.
ISO 9000:2015.

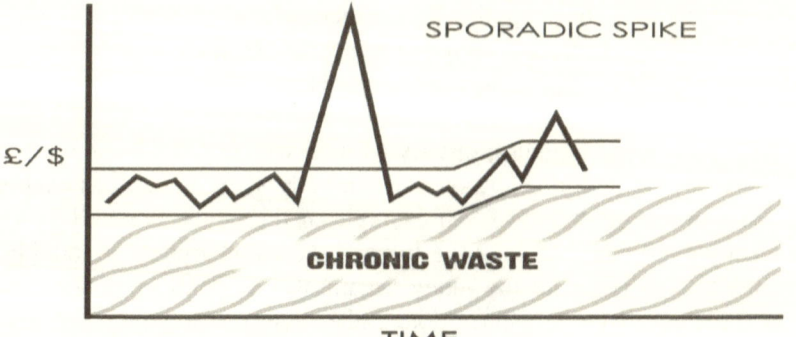

When organisations fail to recognise that "Chronic Waste" is occurring there is every chance that the Chronic Waste will increase as they have no information to deal with it.

Let's remind ourselves that "Chronic Waste" is continuing to carry out an activity in an ineffective manner. It is literally where income continues to hemorrhage and disappear into a Black Hole. In many cases this loss is not even recognised.

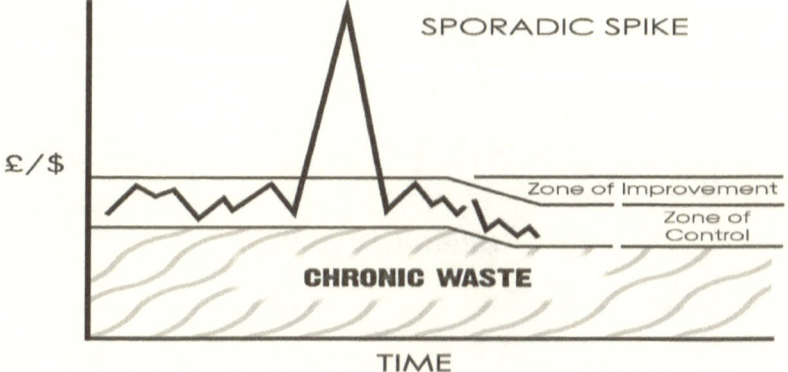

FINANCIAL BLACK HOLES   February 2019

Let's take a further look at how "Chronic Waste" can be dealt with
The above illustrates how improvement can reduce the level of Chronic
Waste. Even small downward movement of the Zone of Control reduces
the amount of "Chronic Waste". The small incremental reduction in
Chronic Waste identified above as the "Zone of Improvement" will
provide ongoing financial saving.

To do this it requires "Information" which means obtaining "Meaningful
Data". Unless leadership obtain meaningful data (Information) no
improvement is possible.

(Attachment E Problem Sheet can be used to obtain information)
Go to www.pdqms.co.uk look under articles to see an A4 Problem Sheet
that can be used.

 FINANCIAL BLACK HOLES   February 2019

3.0 - IMPORTANT VOCABULARY AND DEFINITIONS

There are many instances where quality personnel have not been taught the importance of having a common understanding of the terms used. To understand this book it is important to have a common understanding of the terms and definitions used throughout the book.

The first term, as already mentioned, is **"Chronic Waste"** as it relates to a problem: -

<u>Chronic Waste</u>
Continuing to carry out an activity in an ineffective manner

<u>Audit Trail</u>
A systematic approach to collecting evidence based on specific samples, that the output of a series of inter-related processes meets the expected outcomes

Audit Trail is another term that is not defined anywhere except the ISO Auditing Practices group (Attachment D). Although it has been proposed to the committee responsible for vocabulary it has been rejected as, according to consensus within the committee, it is too difficult to explain. It should be noted that Audit Trail is a requirement within UKAS and IRCA Auditor Examinations. In fact it is impossible to carry out an effective process audit without taking samples and following the audit trail.

The above two terms are not defined within the ISO 9001:2015 Fundamentals and vocabulary covering quality management. This is particularly relevant as many audits are poor and fail to give any confidence that the processes are effective.

The other terms below are from "ISO 9000 Fundamentals and Vocabulary". The ISO 9000 standard is one of the "Core" standards and the central repository for Fundamentals and Vocabulary relating to Quality Management.

10

FINANCIAL BLACK HOLES   February 2019

ISO 9001:2015 Annex B Core Standards

On occasion, this book challenges the latest version and the term preferred is from a previous version rather than the latest. This is because, in some cases, the changes that have been made are unclear. Where that occurs, it is identified with an explanation to help the reader understand why the previous term is preferred. The preferred terms are identified in **bold and underlined**.

Specific Terms used in this book: -

Audit - Systematic, independent and documented process for obtaining **audit evidence and evaluating it objectively** to determine the extent to which audit criteria are fulfilled.
ISO 9000:2005 is the preferred term.

The revised version ISO 9000:2015 now states
Audit - Systematic, independent and documented process for obtaining **objective evidence and evaluating it objectively** to determine the extent to which audit criteria are fulfilled.

FINANCIAL BLACK HOLES   February 2019

Even the definition used in ISO 9000:2015 namely "obtaining objective evidence and evaluating it objectively" is confusing as it has incorrectly used objective to explain objective.

This diagram below shows the difference between Audit Evidence and Objective Evidence

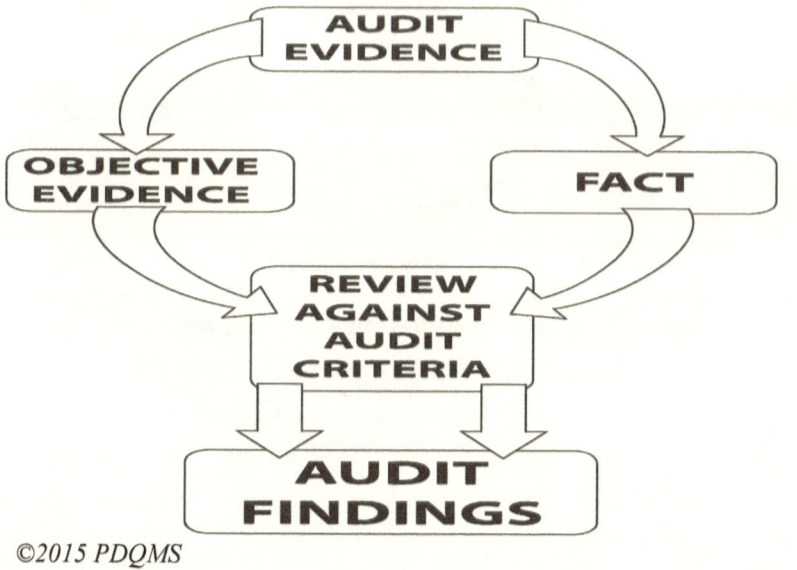

©2015 PDQMS

It is not logical to believe that Audit Evidence and Objective Evidence are the same thing. That is why the diagram shows that Audit Evidence consists of Objective Evidence and Fact. Objective evidence is evidence that can be physically seen. However fact, without evidence, can only be verified with agreement from the auditee because there is no physical evidence available.

ISO 9000:2015 has the following definitions: -

3.9.4 Audit evidence: - records statements of **fact** or other information which are relevant to the audit criteria and verifiable.

3.8.1 Objective evidence: - data supporting the existence or verity (Truth) of something.

As can be seen from the revised definition for Audit in ISO 9000:2015 it incorrectly believes that "Audit Evidence" and "Objective Evidence" are

FINANCIAL BLACK HOLES   February 2019

the same. This belief has allowed the modification to incorrectly change the term Audit Evidence to Objective Evidence.

ISO 9000:2015 Fundamentals and Vocabulary
Audit - Systematic, independent and documented process for obtaining **objective evidence and evaluating it objectively** to determine the extent to which audit criteria are fulfilled.

As can be seen from the above the definition. Audit evidence and objective evidence is different. This is because audit evidence covers both objective evidence and fact.

The four terms **Audit Evidence, Objective Evidence, Audit Criteria** and **Audit Findings** all have specific meanings. The auditor obtains Audit Evidence containing a) Objective evidence, indisputable physical evidence, together with b) fact, something that is true however no actual physically evidence exist. This means it must be agreed with the auditee before it can be confirmed as fact. Then both Objective Evidence and Factual Evidence are referenced against the Audit Criteria to develop the Audit Findings that are presented at the closing meeting.

Audit Criteria
Set of policies, procedures or requirements used as a reference against which Audit evidence is compared. (From previous version ISO 9000:2005)
Audit Criteria
Set of policies, procedures or requirements used as a reference against which objective evidence is compared. ISO 9000:2015

Note: - The later version of Audit Criteria is not preferred as once again Objective Evidence has replaced Audit Evidence in this version.

Audit Findings
Records, statement of fact or other information, which are relevant to the audit criteria and verifiable ISO 9000:2015

There is an interesting change made from the ISO 9000:2005 definition of auditor where it was previously defined as: -

Auditor ISO 9000:2005
Person with the **demonstrated personal attributes and competence** to conduct an audit.

 FINANCIAL BLACK HOLES February 2019

The latest standard now states: -
Auditor ISO 9000:2015
Person who conducts an audit

So in their wisdom, the ISO TC 176 committee covering vocabulary has removed **personal attributes and competence**. It is this approach that undermines quality. It is strongly recommended that organisations ensure that their auditors do have the personal attributes and competence to carry out process audits. Auditing or even carrying out reviews are not about checking the documented system is being followed. It is about seeing if a process achieves the required output. This means that it is necessary to know what the output should be before carrying out the audit/reviews.

To carry out process audits, it is necessary to take selective samples. Then to use those samples to find out what the output would be. Then to follow the audit trail of the samples chosen to see if the process is able to consistently achieve the desired outcome.

From this, it is possible for any auditor that has the **personal attributes and competence** to carry out a professional process audit and be able to judge if the process is effective.

NOTE! The new definitions does not require that!
If you do an audit you are an auditor!

According to the latest definition, if you carry out audits you are an auditor. There is no need to **demonstrate personal attributes and competence.** Why would this phrase be removed?

No wonder audits are struggling to be recognised as an effective measure of whether an **organisation can consistently provide product and services that meet customer and applicable statutory and regulatory requirements.**
 (See ISO 9001 2015 clause 1 Scope)

It should also be noted that the Statutory and Regulatory requirements mentioned above are only those requirements that relate to the product/service provided to the customer. They are not all the statutory and regulatory requirements that the organisation has to comply with.
(See ISO 9001:2015 Clause 1 Scope Note 1)

Is it a good idea to meet customer and relevant legal requirements?

 FINANCIAL BLACK HOLES   February 2019

4.0 - SUMMARY WHERE INEFFECTIVE ACTIVITIES ARE NOT RECOGNISED

The intention is to provide three examples of where organisations activities fail to identify where there are opportunities to make improvements. The following examples contain some issues raised at the 26th World Conference in Las Vegas in April 2018. Following this presentation, delegates provided feedback (Attachment A). The consensus was that there is an opportunity to improve, however, there is a lack of understanding as to how to address the concerns that were raised. Therefore, it requires a "Mind Set" change if this is to have any chance of success. It is hoped that this book could be a catalyst for what needs to be done.

Experience indicates that people do not go to work to provide a poor service. The problem identified is that organisations are locked into their system with no recourse to make them more effective. There are examples where decisions are made that cannot be justified, yet there is no incentive to change what happens as they just follow their system.

The three examples provide a short summary of what has occurred to explain the concern.

4.1 Complaints
This covered a "Review" of the complaints process where a concerned customer had indicated the system was "ineffective".
The review carried out was restricted by the scope which stated: -

- The objective of the review is to ascertain the effectiveness and resilience of the organisations complaint process
- **It is not intended to adjudicate upon any previous or existing complaints**
- The review is conducted by an appointed, independent and suitably experienced reviewing consultant.

This literally meant that the person tasked with conducting the review could not actually look at any actually complaints. The review therefore only consisted of viewing seven documents that were given to them by the organisation under review.

 FINANCIAL BLACK HOLES   February 2019

The independent review concluded that: -
"The organisation has an effective and resilient process in place for receiving and resolving complaints of which the stages and levels are detailed within its process documents and policies, **with no tangible evidence to suggest otherwise".**

What took place was just a "Document review" carried out by an individual appointed by the organisations and carried out at their premises. It is therefore evident that **"there is little tangible evidence to suggest otherwise"** because the assessor did not look at any evidence at all. How can the complaints review achieve the objective of ascertaining the **effectiveness and resilience** of the organisations complaint process, when they did not look at any actual complaints? In fact it was not even possible to ascertain if the organisation had even followed their own procedures let alone see if they were effective.

Conclusion

a) This type of document review cannot actually judge if the process is **effective and resilient** as it has restricted the review to just looking at documents provided by the organisation to the body carrying out the review.

b) This approach does not even ascertain if the organisations personnel are even following their own documented system, never mind see if the process is effective.

What should be done?

This is where the difficulty occurs, if this is the process that is followed and they fail to recognise that anything is wrong, then it is therefore not possible to take "Correction" or "Corrective Action".

This is hindered where senior personnel within the organisation do not recognise that what took place was ineffective.

Therefore nothing can be done as the above is "Unconscious Incompetence" (Attachment C) or even worse a deliberate move to protect the organisation from any criticism.

FINANCIAL BLACK HOLES   February 2019

Major Concern

It is worth noting that the organisation identified in this example trains people in this type of activity. This is why personnel trained by this company feel unable to challenge what they have been taught even if it does seem illogical.

It is the same as the so called "System Audit" where auditors only audit the documented system. Many people believe you cannot audit without a procedure which is untrue. Just auditing the documented system is not effective. What should occur is a "Process Audit" where the auditor takes the time to understand what the output from the process should be before carrying out the audit. Then using that information is able to check to see if the management system being used, including the competence of the personnel, can consistently achieve the desired output.

Opportunity for improvement

This can only be dealt with if it is recognised that the current system would not achieve the objective of the review: - **namely to ascertain the effectiveness and resilience of the organisations complaint process.**

Unless this occurs no changes can take place

FINANCIAL BLACK HOLES   February 2019

4.2 Hedge inspection

When trimmed, hedges, as shown below, can be a nice feature and an amenity however when left uncared for they are a liability

As an illustration the following case study shows a classic situation where an organisation uses a **guidance document** approved by government to justify their decision. Yet when challenged to justify their decision they respond by stating it is government approved.

Here is a hedge that is neatly trimmed at 4 meters

- ▸ The purpose of a hedge is to enable it to screen a garden for privacy
- ▸ It is also sometimes used to screen noise if the hedge is by a road
- ▸ The Local Council are the only recognised body in the UK that can carry out an independent review of a hedge. The council were asked to inspect the hedge because it was being left uncared for

It should be noted that as hedges become taller they are more difficult to keep tidy and special equipment is often needed to trim the hedge.

Because the hedge was not being trimmed a complaint was made using Part 8 of the Anti-Social Behavior Act 2003 High Hedges.

FINANCIAL BLACK HOLES   February 2019

The council were asked to inspect the hedge because it was being left uncared for

The Council report indicated that a height of 3.5 − 4 metres (12.8ft) is acceptable for privacy.

However, using the government approved guidance document issued by the Building Research Establishment, the Council concluded that the actionable height for the hedge is be 11.17 metres (35 feet) **Note: -** This would cover most if not all of the blue sky in the picture.

As the Local Council are the only body in the UK that can make judgements on hedges without going directly to the legal profession they were asked to assess the situation.

▶ The report indicated that a height of 3.5 − 4 metres (12.8ft) is acceptable for privacy.
▶ The council failed to explain, despite being asked on many occasions, what the justification was for increasing the hedge above 4 metres
▶ Eventually the only response received from the Council was they were following government approved guidelines of the Building Research Establishment (BRE).
▶ It was identified that this was a "Guidance document" and the calculation using the BRE document identified the actionable height as 11.17 meters which is unrealistic.
▶ The council were then asked to explain what the purpose was for increasing the height above 4 meters that is acceptable for privacy once again they refused to offer a response.

All the above were justified against the Government approved Guidance document

Due to receiving a rejection the Executive Director of the Council was contacted

The Executive Director of the Council was asked the following two questions: -

1. Could the BRE guidance document allow the hedge to be below 4 metres where there was a small garden involved? **The answer was yes.**

FINANCIAL BLACK HOLES   February 2019

2. Should the BRE guidance document be used to penalise owners of larger gardens?
The answer given categorically stated that it is not the intention to penalise owners of larger gardens.

Therefore this response would indicate there was no justification for increasing the height of the hedge above the 4 metres, however **The Executive Director of the Council indicated that the complaint is closed as they had wasted too much time on this and the Council had followed their system**

The author is aware that there are many complaints about the way councils make decisions. However, it seems there is little recourse available as the councils are able to move the responsibility for the complaint to another government department. Even if the complaint is taken to a legal representative they will only ascertain if the Council have followed their system. Therefore, although the councils system is considered unsuitable by their customers it seems there is no way of getting the Council to justify what they do as they believe they are "Bullet Proof" if they follow their system. The contention is that as Councils have their income secured by Government there is little incentive to improve what they do.

Conclusion

a) There is no incentive to investigate why the complaint has been made

b) There is no recognition of the need to take effective corrective action (See Section 5)

c) Questions raised are sometimes answered however even where they do respond it does not always answer the question that was raised or they ignore the question completely.

d) To date there is still no answer to the question **"On what grounds has the hedge been increased above the 3.5 – 4 meter height recognized in the Councils report as being acceptable for privacy".**

e) Even the objective evidence in the Inspection report was ignored and overruled by the Building Research Establishment document that was not even mentioned in the scope of the report.

FINANCIAL BLACK HOLES   February 2019

Opportunity for improvement

This can only be dealt with if it is recognised that what has occurred cannot be justified. This is where once again difficulty occurs. If the council's processes are being followed and the council staff fail to recognise that anything is wrong then it is not possible to take "Correction" never mind "Corrective Action".

This is hindered where senior personnel within the organisation are not able to justify the decision made yet do not recognise that what took place could be ineffective and costly.

Therefore nothing can be done as the above is "Unconscious Incompetence" (Attachment C) or even worse a deliberate move to protect the organisation from any criticism.

This can only be dealt with if it is recognised that there needs to be a body that does have the responsibility to identify where there is no justification for the decisions being made. The   current system does not achieve the objective of the Anti-Social Behaviour Act.

Unless someone is made accountable nothing will change

What should be done?

The first thing that should be looked at is the number of complaints in this area of activity. This is hindered by the council system where they do not have to register the complaint where it has been taken to another government department. This means that they do not have all of the information needed to be able to analyse what has occurred.

As already mentioned information is key to dealing with problems. Any organisation that does not gather all the information and take the opportunity to investigate why complaints are being made are unlikely to improve.

The situation is confused because another independent government body, that is not part of the council, is now responsible. The organisation that carries out the review are the only ones that can identify how many

 FINANCIAL BLACK HOLES   February 2019

complaints are made and the time spent dealing with this. Even the reviewing body only have the information on the complaints that have been sent to them. The government body that reviews these issues is not allowed to do anything accept see if the council follow their system. I quote from one of the reviewing organisations staff "We do not have the time to see if the councils processes are effective we only check if they have followed their system".

So in effect there is no body within the process that has responsibility for ensuring the processes used are effective and efficient. Even the ombudsman indicates that if the council are following a government approved document then they cannot challenge this.

The answer is that only the government can do anything to improve this process.

Major Concern

All this information has been provided to government ministers and formal responses are still awaited.

 FINANCIAL BLACK HOLES   February 2019

4.3 Grenfell tower fire

The concerns expressed in the previous situation, although different, are illustrated in the "Grenfell Tower" judicial enquiry. Where once again the Council is possibly being defended by extending the scope beyond what is required.

In this example it illustrates that this type of judicial enquiry can be managed in a manner that reduces the ability to identify the "Root Cause" of the problem. It shows how easy it is to extend the scope to include issues not relevant to the refurbishment of Grenfell Tower.

In this example the Scope provided has been broadened by increasing the issues that have to be considered. This approach fails to focus the enquiry on how well the Council managed the refurbishment of Grenfell Tower.

This cannot be gone into too much detail as the formal enquiry is still to be finalized by the Government appointed enquiry. Concern was raised about the manner in which the enquiry would be carried out and these concerns were provided (Attachment B) to the local MP in June 2017. The judge, appointed to carry out this Review, indicated that, from the terms of reference he was given, he would not be able to satisfy all the people who were affected by the fire. The question that should be asked is about how the contract was approved and controlled including how sub-contractors were appointed and the relevant regulatory and legislation applicable at that time. (Bold scope below)

Actual Scope provided to the Grenfell Tower enquiry
- ▶ To examine the circumstances around the fire
    - ◦ The immediate cause and why the fire spread
    - ◦ Design and construction of the building
    - ◦ **Decisions relating to its modification & refurbishment**
    - ◦ The scope and adequacy of the building
    - ◦ **Whether the regulations and legislation were complied with**
    - ◦ **Arrangements made by the local authority**
    - ◦ Fire and safety measures at Grenfell tower
    - ◦ Response of the London Fire Brigade and local government
- ▶ To report the findings to the prime minister

FINANCIAL BLACK HOLES   February 2019

Extending the scope beyond the primary concern of how the Council, responsible for the refurbishment, controlled and managed the processes may be why the enquiry has not yet been completed. (Some 18 Months plus after the enquiry started)

This problem of extending the scope is demonstrated when the enquiry asked the Senior Fire Officer, who was first on the scene, why he did not immediately evacuate the building?

The answer is simple the current system relied on the building being refurbished to the correct specification as it **SHOULD** have been safer to keep residents in their apartments.

The author's contention is that what should take place is a straight forward **Professional Process Audit/Review** where the scope restricts itself to just covering the refurbishment of the Grenfell Tower. (See clarification meeting with MP 30th June 2017 Attachment B)

Yes there are other issues of concern but it should be remembered that it is necessary, when something goes wrong, to ascertain the "Root Cause" of the problem.

From the reports published in the Times newspaper dated 30th June 2017 there were various issue's raised that need to be investigated. It is important to understand what occurred was, according to the Times, possibly caused by the manner in which the refurbishment of the Grenfell Tower was carried out.

As mentioned in the following 2 page document presented to the local Member of Parliament on the 30th June 2017 (Attachment B) there were specific statements made, by the Times newspaper, on the day of the scheduled meeting with the Member of Parliament that stated and I quote: -

a) Fireproof cladding planned for Grenfell Tower was downgraded to save £293,000 as housing officials demanded "good costs" to satisfy a council boss, leaked emails revealed.

24

FINANCIAL BLACK HOLES   February 2019

b) There was also another statement that reductions of the cladding costs were among savings of £ 693,000 required from the main contractor, Rydon, **(After it had been selected?)**

The above and other issues raised cause significant concerns about the process.

JOHN RUSKIN

The common law of business prohibits paying a little and getting a lot. It can't be done. If you deal with the lowest bidder its well to add something for the risk you run and if you do that you will have enough to pay for something better

John Ruskin – 1819 - 1900

Still valid today

Primary concern?

Was the refurbishment of the Grenfell Tower carried out to the required specification for a building of this type and were the statutory and regulatory requirements applicable at that time complied with?

The actual document provided during the meeting with the MP 30th June 2017 Attachment B.

It should be noted that the Times newspaper dated 30th June 2017 was used to expand on the issues raised from the previous submission sent to the MP on the 28th June 2017 that triggered the meeting.

Conclusion
a) The priority was to carry out a refurbishment at a low cost
b) It seems as if even after the contract had been approved the winning contractor was asked to look at carrying out the job at an even lower price
c) The scope as given to the responsible party carrying out the enquiry indicated that it would not be possible to satisfy those people affected by the fire.

25

FINANCIAL BLACK HOLES   February 2019

d) The scope should have concentrated on the refurbishment of the Grenfell tower and how that was managed. Information available from the articles in the press gave significant cause for concern over the manner this was carried out.

Opportunity for improvement

This is where the difficulty occurs. If the individuals involved failed to recognise that having a main focus on reduction of cost without ensuring the suitability of the material being used then their ability to make these decisions should have been challenged.

What should be done?

The enquiry may have benefited from having three different teams using modified scopes. Having a scope that has tried to cover everything will always delay the time frame for the report. The suggested approach would be to have three teams each tackling a specific issue that need to be considered regarding the Grenfell Tower Fire.

This example is restricted to using the actual scope provided to the enquiry team.

Example: -

a) The first is to ascertain if the refurbishment by the council was carried out in an effective manner that met all the legal requirements applicable at the time of the refurbishment were complied with.
   a. **Decisions relating to its modification & refurbishment**
   b. **Whether the regulations and legislation were complied with**
   c. **Arrangements made by the local authority**

b) To examine the circumstances around the fire
   a. The immediate cause and why the fire spread
   b. Design and construction of the building

c) To report on the building and its use
   a. The scope and adequacy of the building
   b. Fire and safety measures at Grenfell tower

FINANCIAL BLACK HOLES   February 2019

    c. Response of the London Fire Brigade and local government

Note: - All of the above are from the scope of the enquiry and the detail in the text has not been altered. There may be other issues that need to be included to cover everything.

Major Concern

The enquiry has still not been finalized. The concerns raised on the 30th June 2017 by the author and provided to the government highlighted concerns about how effective the enquiry would be. This was because some reports indicated that price was a major factor and the scope, when obtained, was too broad. It needed the root cause to be identified and it needed information on how well the refurbishment had been handled. The first example of scope, above, could have been completed within three months using an independent team of four professional auditors.

There is still no report and the fact that the person leading the enquiry indicated that he would not be able to satisfy those affected by the fire is of concern. (see Times newspaper report dated the 30th June 2017) Concerns raised from the information in the Times can be seen in attachment B.

The fact that this is now over 18 months ago will make it difficult to assess what went on at that time.

 FINANCIAL BLACK HOLES   February 2019

5.0 - SUMMARY WHERE INEFFECTIVE ACTIVITY HAS BEEN RECOGNISED

Please note that I would like to thank those organisations that recognised they were responsible for providing an ineffective service. This is where the Organisations accepted that something had gone wrong with what they had done. It would be tedious to put in all the detail, therefore this contains some short examples of what occurred.

Prior to looking at this it is important to understand three terms that are defined in ISO 9000:2015 Fundamentals and Vocabulary and how they have been used in these scenario to see which term is relevant: -

3.12.3 Correction
Action to eliminate a detected non conformity
- This is literally to put things right nothing more. It can consist of a replacement product or service or even financial payment or other method of satisfying the customer

3.12.2 Corrective Action
Action to eliminate the cause of a nonconformity to prevent recurrence
- This requires the organisations to identify why something has gone wrong and modify what takes place to ensure it does not happen again

3.12.1 Preventive action
Action to eliminate the cause of a potential nonconformity or other undesirable situation
- **This happens before something goes wrong** and this was introduced in the year 2000 based on the "Vision 2000" sub-committee work investigation into where ISO 9001 could be improved. It was in ISO 9001 2000 that the need for preventive action was introduced. Prior to the 2000 the ISO 9001 standard waited for things to go wrong before any action was taken.

FINANCIAL BLACK HOLES   February 2019

As can be seen failure to understand these terms has led to misunderstanding over their meaning. In fact the USA used a term known as "CAPA" standing for "Correction Action" "Preventive Action". This term led people to believe that the "Preventive Action" was what happened to resolve Corrective Action. As can be seen from above this was wrong,

5.1 A Credit Card Company (CCC)

This is where an organisation had introduced a new phone in payments process that did not work. In this example there was a facility to pay by phone and a request to pay £ 600 was made. The credit card company (CCC) stated that the payment had been declined so a second payment of £ 300 was suggested in case the figure had been too high, however that payment was also declined.

The Credit Card holder made a visit to his bank where both payments had actually been authorized. Copies of both authorization details were provided by the bank. The bank also indicated that both the £ 600 and the £ 300 authorities were valid and could be actioned at any time by the Credit Card Company. A letter was written to the CCC containing the banks authorised documents. It asked the CCC to cancel both of the authorised amounts. This was due to the fact that it would have caused the customers bank account to be overdrawn.

This took months to resolve and during that time a credit card statement was received with a penalty payment. Once again contact was made and it was agreed that £ 100 compensation plus a return of the penalty payment would be made.

It became obvious that this was only a **"Correction"** because the next credit card statement once again had a penalty payment added. This led to another letter being written and an email was received offering a further £ 50 plus the return of the penalty payment.

The reason this is mentioned is that it highlights the difference between a **"Correction"** where something is put right and **"Corrective Action"** that investigates what went wrong and takes action to stop it happening again.

This is a typical example of "Chronic Waste" shown in chapter 2. This waste becomes a steady drain of the income of the organisation. In fact this

FINANCIAL BLACK HOLES   February 2019

becomes a normal part of the process within the CCC as personnel believe that there is nothing that can be done about it.

5.2 Monthly Debit payment for Lawn Treatment

This was where a monthly debit payment was made and the organisation carrying out the lawn treatment were asked to cancel the monthly Direct Debit and go back to only paying for treatment specified by the house owner. They failed to stop this monthly payment.
Once again this was recognised as a fault on their side and they repaid the money they had taken and offered a free aeration treatment in recognition of the error on their part.

Result: - It was certainly a **"Correction"** with some compensation for the inconvenience to the customer. However, it could only be "Corrective Action" if the system was changed in a manner that prevented the problem happening again. The current situation is not known.

The reason this is included is to mention the need to capture this information so that a review can take place to ascertain if the error has become a regular occurrence. How many times has this occurred? What needs to be done to prevent this happening again?

5.3 Booking Accommodation on line

This is where a family of 6 including a child were booked into an apartment in Los Angeles. When they arrived, they were advised by the duty manager that the apartments are for residents only and could not be sub-let out. The manager was very helpful and as it was too late to locate another apartment, however after 3 hours searching, a hotel was booked. All of this was reported to the online booking agency and they asked for invoices. The hotel invoices were provided however no receipt for the two taxis were obtained. The two taxi journeys came to $ 100. The booking agency believed that as the hotel was a similar cost to the apartment, they did not have to pay any fees for change to the hotel. It was explained to the booking Agency that the apartment would have allowed the family to make their own breakfast and meals without having to go elsewhere as the Hotel rooms had no facilities to do so.

The initial offer was $ 50 as there were no receipts for the Taxi's. It was explained that as this was a holiday, it is not normal to ask for receipts. The offer of $ 50 was rejected. After a considerable amount of time, where

FINANCIAL BLACK HOLES   February 2019

numerous members of staff were involved, it was agreed that an inconvenience payment would be made that was more acceptable to the family. This again highlights the wasted time spent by the agency in dealing with this. It is this type of defensive approach that is part of the "Chronic Waste" within an organisations activities.

The reason this is included is because it was investigated by the family to see if that particular apartment was still being offered by the online agency. It was found that it was indeed still being advertised. Although a financial **"Correction"** had taken place there was no **"Corrective Action"** carried out. This was despite the agency being advised that the apartments were only to be used by residents and owners were not allowed to sub-let the apartments. The fact that the apartments were still being offered for rent indicates that the **"Root Cause"**, although identified, was not dealt with to ensure other customers would not experience the same problem,

The above is a very short summary of what the family had experienced. Even on return home, the number of different people within the agency that had to be sent information was considerable. It was also difficult to see if all personnel involved with this complaint had been given all the information that had been sent in. Therefore it was some months before there was full recognition of the inconvenience to the family and the complaint was recognised.

Result: - It seems as if it was only **"Correction"** that had taken place. This consisted of a financial payment for the inconvenience to the customer. It could be "Corrective Action" only if the system was changed in a manner that prevented it happening again. It has not been possible to check if "Corrective Action" has occurred however it is never too late to turn the "Correction" into "Corrective Action" provided information had been obtained. The opportunity for improvement, by taking "Corrective Action", was possibly missed because, although they had the information on why the apartment could not be let out, the online booking system failed to remove the apartment from their listing.

This is a typical example of "Chronic Waste" as they could have the same problem again.

Where an organisation only carried out "Correction". It may keep them within the zone of control however this means they are not taking action to reduce chronic waste.

FINANCIAL BLACK HOLES February 2019

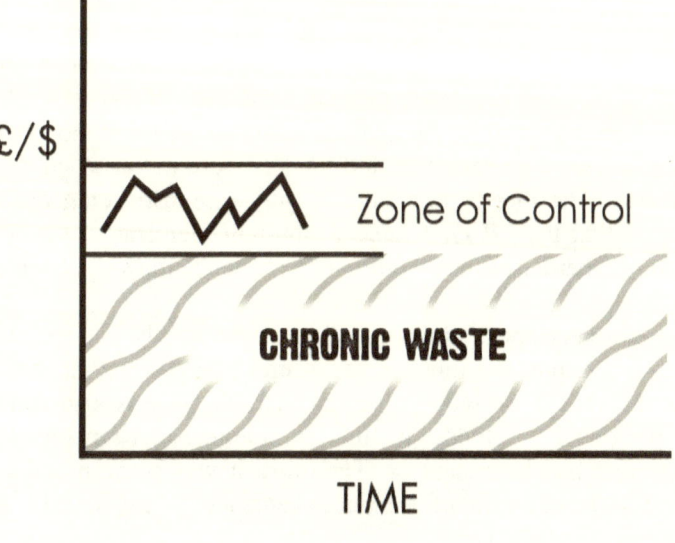

FINANCIAL BLACK HOLES   February 2019

6.0 - SUMMARY OF EXAMPLES GIVEN

The previous 2 sections of the book (Sections 4 and 5) were introduced to give readers some examples of actual instances where problems were not effectively dealt with.

Section 4 Non acceptance of a problem

The three examples of where an organisation does not believe it has failed to achieve the desired result is intended to highlight how organisations can continue doing the same thing without recognising that they could improve the management system if they investigated the complaints in a professional manner.

Failing to recognise that there is a problem, leaves the organisation open to the same thing happening again because they have not identified the cause of the problem and taken action to stop it happening again

Section 5 Acceptance that something was incorrectly carried out

The three examples where the organisations did accept that what they had done did not meet the customer's requirements. Therefore were undermined as they only carried out "Correction". The reason for the concern is that there was no definitive example where the root cause had been identified and action taken to ensure that the same mistake could not occur again.

Recognising that there is a problem but failure to ensure it does not happen again is why organisations have a large proportion of "Chronic Waste".

HAVE DOCUMENTS OVERRULLED COMMON SENSE?

 FINANCIAL BLACK HOLES   February 2019

READERS VIEW?

The above short summary has been introduced as it was felt that it would be worth pausing here and allow readers time to think about what their own organisation do?

- Does your organisation take corrective action or just carry out correction when problems occur?

- Does your organisation gather information on the problems experienced?

- Does your organisation use a system that enables it to improve and reduce complaints?

- Is there anybody in your organisation who has the responsibility, authority and accountability to gather information and take "Corrective Action".

FINANCIAL BLACK HOLES   February 2019

7.0 - HOW TO IMPROVE

To begin with it is necessary to try to understand what the human issues are that may affect what takes place. (See Attachment Competence model.) In section 4, the three examples mainly demonstrate **"Unconscious Incompetence"** where the individual is unaware of their lack of skills and knowledge to work efficiently and effectively. (See Attachment C)

In section 5 there are examples of where the organisation have recognised errors, however it is unclear if they have taken action to stop the same problem happening again.

7.1 Responsibilities, Authorities and Accountability

There is a lot of information about **Responsibility** which has been around for centuries. During the 20th century, **Authority** was pushed as in many cases, people had responsibility but little authority. It has to be stated that authority is still not always recognised or clear. The modern problem is

Accountability.

The terms above are covered within the competency framework.

COMPETENCY FRAMEWORK

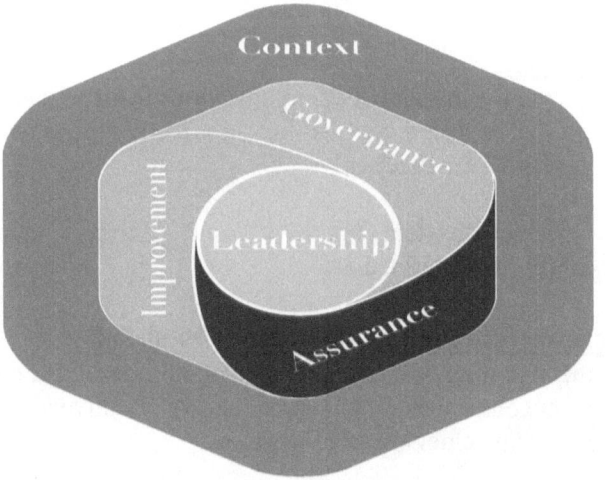

The new competency framework recently introduced by the Chartered Quality Institute (CQI) and Confederation of British Industry (CBI) is a high level approach on how an organisation should manage its activities. Detailed information can be obtained for the (CQI) based in London.

FINANCIAL BLACK HOLES   February 2019

The text below is a very **simplistic** explanation of the terms: -

7.2 CONTEXT

This covers the circumstances that form the setting in which the organization works. It is important that leadership understand everything that can affect their ability to meet customer requirements. It covers what they do and any issues that can impact on their ability to carry out those activities, even those issues that are not in their direct control need to be considered. This includes all interested parties that can impact or affect or impede their ability to achieve the desired outcome. It is essential that the organisation takes into account all relevant Statutory and Regulatory requirements (Legal) that are applicable to their activities both within the country they work in and the countries their products or services are provided to.

7.3 LEADERSHIP

Is, as represented, the central core of the competency framework. Without a clear understanding of how to manage the Governance, Assurance and Improvement there is little chance of demonstrating competence.

This is where authority, responsibility and accountability reside. Unfortunately this is not always dealt with in an effective manner.

7.4 ASSURANCE

This is the manner in which organisations manage their business. It covers the importance of having an effective management system and is critical for success.

The phrase "System approach" and "Process approach" has previously been defined as: -

System approach to management (ISO 9000:2005)

Identifying, understanding and managing interrelated processes as a system contributes to the organization's effectiveness and efficiency in achieving its objectives.

FINANCIAL BLACK HOLES   February 2019

Process approach (ISO 9000:2005)

A desired result is achieved more efficiently when activities and related resources are managed as a Process

As can be seen from the two terms above, they clearly define the difference between system and process. They explain how the processes are managed as a system to ensure they interact and work in harmony to achieve the desired result.

These above two terms were introduced by the TC176 Sc2 sub group work carried out in early 1990's. The sub-committee work became known as "Vision 2000". The above terms were introduced in the year 2000 revision as the **"ISO 9000 Family of standards"** where it identified the eight management principles. These management principles have now been reduced to seven within ISO 9000:2015.

7.5 GOVERNANCE

This covers how an organisation controls and manages all the relevant interrelated processes within the management system that enables the organisation to function in an effective manner. It needs to cover the accountability of the organisations activities if activities are to be improved.

More detailed information can be obtained from the CQI.

The above has been introduced because in too many cases organisations hide behind their systems. There are many instances where an organisation indicates that they will revise their system so that the undesirable result will not occur again. Unfortunately experience shows that statements made are often not achieved as the problem reoccurs.

How can an organisation improve if the same people are left in charge and no effort is made to retrain them? What often takes place is a "Correction" and in many cases the root cause is not identified. Where this occurs it is termed **"Unconscious Incompetence"** (See Attachment C) where the individual carrying out the role does not understand enough about what is being done to recognise that what is happening is not effective.

37

 FINANCIAL BLACK HOLES   February 2019

USING THE SAME PEOPLE AND EXPECTING A DIFFERENT RESULT IS ILLOGICAL

7.6 IMPROVEMENT

This is an essential requirement for any competency framework. To stand still in today's fast moving world would mean falling behind to the extent that the business could fail. The need to meet customer expectations and have an acceptable cost is crucial for organisation to stay viable. If an organization has a sound method of reducing waste they will ensure that the hemorrhage of income will be reduced. This in turn will reduce the "Chronic Waste".

Preventive action is something that is done before a problem is experienced.

Preventive Action ISO 9000 2015
Action taken to eliminate the causes of potential nonconformity or other potential undesirable situation

It has been unfortunate that the removal of "Preventive action" from the revised ISO 9001:2015, first introduced into ISO 9001 2000 by the "Vision 2000" sub-committee, has meant that the purpose of the procedure, which was to provide all personnel with the opportunity to highlight areas that they believed might cause a problem has been lost.

The replacement term "Risk Based Thinking" is not properly taught or understood. In fact the whole purpose of the ISO 9001 has always been to reduce risk by having an effective management system. The problem with this is too many people have been taught that a management system means a documented system and that is not true. The only way to understand what the term "Risk Based Thinking" means is to recognise the restrictive role of ISO 9001. Namely the ability of the management system to demonstrate the organisations ability to consistently provide product and services that meet customer and applicable statutory and regulatory requirements. When this is understood, it is simple to apply "Risk Based Thinking".

In fact the revision to ISO 9001 2015 no longer calls up any specific procedures as it has been left with the organisations leadership to decide what is required.

38

FINANCIAL BLACK HOLES   February 2019

8.0 - AUDITING

The information on auditing is a sample taken from the book ISO 9001 Audit Trail second edition published in October 2012 ISBN 978-1-4772-3489-1 (SC)

What is an Audit Trail?

There is still no definition published in ISO 9000:2015 for Audit Trail yet it is essential for auditors to carry out process audits following an Audit Trail if audits are to be effective.

There are however two versions published: -

- A systematic approach to collecting evidence based on specific samples, that the output of a series of interrelated processes meets the expected outcomes.

This was modified by the International Standards Organisations (ISO) auditing practices group. (See Attachment D)

- An examination, by a qualified person, of an activity following the path that has been left by the process (See Attachment G Part 1)

The second version was from the 1st Edition of ISO 9001 Audit Trail dated March 2010

As explained in the definition it allows a path left by the process or the interrelated processes to be followed to judge if the process being used is able to consistently achieve the desired output.

a). A simple example of this could be that the Organisations purchase order being audited requires a Material Certificate for a bought in item. When the Auditor asks to see this Certificate they can only offer an alternative as they can't find the one for that particular order. This is of course not acceptable as the TRAIL being pursued requires the certificate for the specific order being followed. Even if they had the correct certificate, there is more for the auditor to do, how do they control the certificate? How is it received, identified and stored? Does it retain its link to the product itself? If it needs to be passed to the customer how is this

39

FINANCIAL BLACK HOLES February 2019

managed? What records are kept? The Audit Trail approach would follow this process through to ensure it is consistently controlled and applied.

b) You are auditing a Main Car Dealers Servicing department from taking the order for a car to be serviced to returning the car, fully serviced to the required service level. In this process, a sample of cars being serviced are chosen as the representative sample. These are chosen at the start of the audit and the process for servicing these cars will be followed. You would include a car nearing completion plus others as time allows. You would obtain the job numbers or car numbers to identify how the work has been scheduled. The next thing to check what service was required. Was the service agreed with the customer, does this match the mileage, what was the previous mileage and date of service? Check if the service chosen is correct by checking the service level chosen (10k –20k - 40k etc.) Identify what information the organisation has on what is required for each service. How is this document controlled? Is it a formal manufacturers standard service level (Check-list) for each of the recognised service levels? Or is it just their own version? If it is their own version, how was this devised? Where did the information come from? How do they ensure they have the latest version of this document? Were there any extra requirements that the customer had advised the organisation of? How are these requirements passed to the technician carrying out that service? How are the spares passed to the technician for them to be used in the service? Can the spares issued be cross-referred to the spares fitted? Can they be identified as the actual spares taken from the store? Is this stock or has it been ordered in? Go through the actual material used and verify that this is correct for that make and that version of car. Throughout this process you check the procedures/work instructions etc. to see if the process would ensure the requirements are met. However the audit is not just to see the documented process is being followed, but that the process itself is robust and would indeed ensure the correct information is available. This only covers part of what is required as it has not even touched on the actual work being carried but hopefully it illustrates what is expected from a professional audit. Remember the audit is NOT just auditing to see if the procedures are being followed but checking to see if the process being used is able to consistently achieve the required outcome.

Without taking it further these examples are to show how the process is followed ensuring that all the linked activities for each chosen sample is, when audited, able to objectively demonstrate that the Management System being used can consistently meet the specified

FINANCIAL BLACK HOLES   February 2019

*requirements. From now on the auditing example will be for a motor
dealers organisation.*

**Note: - The term "Management System" does not mean "Documented
System". An effective management system may just require competent
people with no procedures.**

8.1 How to prepare for an audit

The scope and the time frame for the audit is normally specified by the
person requiring the audit (The Originator). The objective of the audit
should also be defined. The first task is to make contact with the
organisation/s giving them a rough time scale e.g. sometime in August
2018. This is especially important where there are a number of
organisations being audited in a country or at different locations.

Once contact has been made with the auditee's organisation, the "contact"
the auditor will be dealing with will be identified. This is the person that
will act as the liaison with the auditor. The initial information needed will
include: -

- What is the normal working week and do they work shifts?
- What is the start and finish times for the day and shift workers?
- What are the times for lunch and are there set times for any breaks
  in the day?
- Does all the work take place at this location? Are there other
  locations?
- Will access be available to all areas? (Secret or Confidential)
- Any safety requirements (Can they provide PPE)?
- Where they are located, how easy is it to get to them and best
  route?
- Plus any other information the auditor may need.

8.2 Audit Programme: -

**ISO 9000:2015 (3.13.4) set of one or more audits planned for a specific
time frame and directed towards a specific purpose.**

The above information is needed to organise this programme and the time
needed to develop this should not be underestimated especially if it
involves different countries, flights, hotels etc. The programme in simple
terms is on what days will Organisations be audited taking into account
travel arrangements.

FINANCIAL BLACK HOLES   February 2019

Note to Auditor WHEN PLANNING AND CONDUCTING THIS TOUR THERE MAY BE ADDITIONAL FACTORS TO CONSIDER eg: political/security issues, culture, health hazards and reduced safety standards.

AUDIT PROGRAMME FOR TRIP TO   XXXXXX

AUDITOR   Luke Around   DATE :   13th – 18th XXXX

			Enter details of chargeable days					
		Company + Mancode	Activity			Travel Details		
Date	Days	Or Location(s)	Travel	Audit	Other (specify	Mode	Depart	Arrive
13		Manchester - Dublin	X			Flight	0800	0855
13		Dublin - Galway	X			Car	10.00	13.00
14	1	Company A Galway		X				
15	1	Company B Shannon		X				
16		Shannon - Dublin	X			Car	18.00	23.00
17	1	Company C Dublin		X				
18	1	Company C Dublin		X				
18		Dublin - Manchester	X			Flight	20.50	21.40

It should be noted that the scope of the audit and the number of audit days should be given as soon as contact is made. On agreement an Audit Plan should be set up : -

 FINANCIAL BLACK HOLES February 2019

8.3 Audit plan: -
ISO 9000:2015 (3.13.6): -Description of the activities and arrangements for an audit.
This will be a document that indicates the start time and activities that will take place. It usually covers departments and timings only. It normally follows the process in a structured manner that enables the auditor to follow the activities sequentially ending with the time for the closing meeting.

It should be noted that the Plan is following the process, <u>NOT</u> the ISO 9001 clauses.
The attached Audit Plan **(See Appendix F)** is a simplified summary running through the audit process demonstrating how to link the plan to an Audit trail.

All auditing whether they are 1st Party, 2nd Party or 3rd Party should ensure that the process is able to consistently achieve the specified requirements. The Internal audit process should, if it is to be beneficial, include interfaces between departments. Each internal audit normally covers a small part of the full process.

It is important that Internal Audits should also be an audit of the process following an Audit Trail and this requires the auditor to have knowledge of what each process should achieve.

Management may also include Internal Audits that are not directly related to the product or service provided. These audits can also be carried out against ISO 9001 requirements however they may not need to be directly audited by certification bodies whose primary auditing role is to see if the organisation can consistently meet the product or service specification. Audits that are solely planned against the clauses of ISO 9001 are NOT effective in demonstrating compliance with the specification.

8.4 How to start the audit
Auditors should always remember why the audit is taking place and what the scope is. The primary purpose of an audit is to ensure that the processes being audited are capable of consistently meeting the specified requirements. It should be noted that it is impossible for a 2nd or 3rd Party auditor to carry out a Professional Audit of an organisation unless the auditor takes the time to understand the specification of the product/service required, including any statutory and regulatory requirements that relate to the product/service itself. It is this professional approach to auditing that

FINANCIAL BLACK HOLES February 2019

allows the auditor to identify the strengths and weaknesses in the process, deciding if that organisation is capable of consistently meeting those specified requirements.

Internal audits should also follow an audit trail, however the audit scope is normally just a small part of the overall process. All of these audits need the auditor to know what the requirements are for the process being audited and should verify that the process with its controls and systems is able to achieve those requirements.

Note: A good approach is to use a form that captures all the names and roles of everyone seen during the audit. It should also identify who attended the opening and closing meeting. (This is useful information when, towards the end of the audit, the training records are checked as this enables personnel from the list to be sampled and checked against the activities they were actually seen doing during the audit.)

Opening Meeting

An opening meeting is always carried out. This is to go over what has been discussed during the planning and is the opportunity to explain what the audit is about. The opening meeting is intended to set the scene for the audit and explain the approach that will be taken: -

- Introductions
- Confirmation of scope and objectives
- Confirm the Audit Plan is still acceptable (Should be sent and agreed before the audit)
- Ensure timings are still suitable
- Any "Special" concerns that could affect the audit. Fire drills, Management meetings etc
- It gives the opportunity to remind the meeting attendees what you are there to achieve. You advise them that you are their to help identify the good practices as well as identify whether there are any weaknesses in their system.
- You confirm the time of the closing meeting and confirm how the findings will be reported at the end of the meeting
- Then give all attendees the opportunity to ask any questions they may have.

Note 1: - The above will already have been discussed with the organisations representative
Note 2: - people are often nervous your role is to ensure they understand you are there to help.

FINANCIAL BLACK HOLES   February 2019

8.5 How to audit

It is important to prepare an Audit Plan that is given to the organisation prior to the visit for their review, to give them an idea of which departments you will be visiting and when. Please refer (Attachment F) at the back of this part of the book for an example of an Audit Plan. Professional Auditors will normally do a walk through the plant to see the location of the departments, visiting the area where the finished article, product or service is being finalised ready for despatch. This enables the auditor to see what's actually taking place and at that time identify job or contract numbers that are being worked on. From this information it is an easy task to go back to the service reception area and identify the agreed requirements for that specific product or service. This is the starting point and allows relevant samples to be chosen. In the case of a car service, the cars identity is a chosen starting point so that the process can be checked to ensure what takes place is controlled and will meet the service requirements. This therefore has been identified as the starting point of the audit. Example used to demonstrate this audit approach is "Top Down" after having identified and chosen a number of samples from the walk around.

From this starting point, the "Audit Trail" is selected and followed through. It is normal to take a sample. The term, "Random Sample" is often used by auditors, however, it is better to use "Selective" or "Representative Sample" as this is what is actually insinuated. (See Attachment G Guidance note Part 5 Selective Sample).

For a 2nd party audit, identifying a similar or identical result to the product or service that is required. For a third party auditor, it means the product identified in their certified scope, noting any exclusions. This is therefore NOT a totally Random Sample.

For internal audits it is what is happening at that time.

When the samples have been chosen (Note: - one is not normally considered a suitable sample). The minimum suggested is three but can be more, however, it does of course depend on the number of days (Time) allowed for the audits and it is not always possible to follow all chosen samples through from beginning to end. It also depends on the complexity of the product or service being provided and the scope of the audit given as this may only cover one contract. It is important to realise that samples are taken throughout the auditing process e.g. Purchase Orders sampled must relate to that particular job (Contract) and the number chosen is up to the

45

FINANCIAL BLACK HOLES   February 2019

auditor. The number of samples chosen should be sufficient to enable the auditor to be confident that the system is working, or not.

Primary and Secondary Processes

Feedback from the First Edition of the March 2010 Audit Trail book indicated that there was little mention of Secondary Processes.

So let's look at both the Primary process and the Secondary support processes in more detail as they will be included in the example used to show how a process audit following an audit trail is carried out.

In some Organisations they have more than one Primary Process especially if they make different products or provide different services.

In fact the main Objective of ISO 9001 is to give confidence to both the Organisation and the Customer that their management system is robust and can consistently meet the required specification. In this example, as already explained, we will concentrate on car servicing and ignore any other activity such as car sales.

Primary Process

The ISO 9001 standard requires Organisations to: -
- Determine the Processes and their application throughout the Organisation Determine their sequence and interactions
- Determine the criteria and methods of control
- May include a description of these in the Quality Manual although this is no longer specified within ISO 9001 2015 as a requirement (Normally Primary) it is still useful to explain what an organisation does.

The primary process is normally covered in ISO 9001 clause 8 Operation ably supported by the secondary processes as appropriate.

Organisation often develop high level flow charts that are used to illustrate the primary processes. Although actually using a flow charts is not an ISO requirement, a simple list of activities that follow the process is equally acceptable. It is up to the Organisation to decide what is most appropriate.

The primary process is the process that is used to ensure that the product or service meets the specified requirements by using a Quality Management System (QMS) that controls the process in a consistent and effective manner.

FINANCIAL BLACK HOLES   February 2019

Let us look at an example of a Primary process: -

1. Approved Supplier List

This activity can be considered a Primary Process.

The reason the Approved Supplier List (ASL) has been chosen is because this area is often poorly audited. The purpose of the audit is not to see if they have an approved supplier list and tick it off the list of requirements, but to see if the process used in developing this list can give information on the credibility and the reliability of the suppliers or contractors being used. Once again, in good audit style, a sample of suppliers or contractors are chosen linked to the relevant sample of jobs chosen on the "Walk Around" or from the list of jobs going through that day. There is no point just looking at any item bought in from a supplier as you need to link this to the sample of cars that were chosen. From this information, it should be possible to check that the suppliers being used were on the ASL and if so, what criteria were used to put them there? If it is as a result of previous good supply – check some evidence, or if it is as a result of supplier audit – have a look at the audit report. It is widely known that using a poor supplier or contractor can have a significant effect on the ability to meet the customer's requirements. One of the most significant problems experienced here is that if there is no information on the individual suppliers listed on the ASL it can invariably lead to orders being placed with the lowest bidder. Historical record on past performance is a powerful indication of whether a supplier can meet the specified requirements where it is "weighted," this can be used in the decision making process.

The information supporting the ASL can be in the form of: -

General Supplier/Vendor information
- Are they ISO 9001 certified and is the certificate valid?
- Who is the Certification and Accreditation Body?
- What is the scope of their certification
- Does it cover the intended supplier/contractor location?
- Is there supplier capability questionnaire available?

For previously used suppliers: -
- Was previous orders delivered in time?
- Did the previous orders meet the specified requirement?
- Did your Organisation have to inspect the goods on receipt?

FINANCIAL BLACK HOLES   February 2019

- Have any items from that supplier been rejected
- Were there any price variations?
- Etc

If the organisation does not have information on the Contractor or Supplier that can be used in the bid analyses process then, as already stated, it puts into doubt the validity of the decision making process.

Secondary Processes

Secondary Processes are not specifically mentioned except by clause requirements outside ISO 9001 section 8 but they support the Primary Process. These Secondary processes are too many to list and are, in effect, any activity that supports the Primary Processes.

Let us look at an example of a Secondary process: -

2. Resources ISO 9001 2015 Clause 7.1

A good technique as already mentioned, is to make a note of the individuals seen during the audit of the Primary Process and what each individual was doing (Job Role). From this list of personnel a sample is taken and used to determine how the competence of those personnel was established. The sample taken can then be judged against what they were actually seen doing. In this way, checking if competent personnel were employed at those stations. This takes in training or other actions to demonstrate competence and the effectiveness of the actions taken. It is important, in this process, to ensure appropriate records of education, training, skills and experience are developed and maintained. Once again, to do this effectively, it is necessary to audit the process that is being used to judge how effectively this is controlled and managed. This is carried out by following an audit trail to demonstrate that the personnel from the sample chosen are competent to do what they are being asked to do. An additional check of their competence may be carried out by checking the likes of non-conformance records and customer complaints to see if there is any correlation between their activities and if this can be linked to lack of competence of any individuals.

As previously indicated, it is not the intention here to go through every primary or secondary process, however it is hoped that the above examples will go some way towards explaining how auditing may also include secondary processes that directly impact or support the Primary Process. It

48

 FINANCIAL BLACK HOLES   February 2019

again emphasises the importance of auditing a process following an Audit Trail. It also emphasises the importance of taking relevant samples and following those samples through, to ensure that the system in place can consistently achieve the required outcome.

Other processes
It should be recognised that there are also activities that are not directly primary processes or even secondary processes used to support the primary process. These activities are often looked at right at the beginning of the audit after the opening meeting (See Attachment F Audit Plan).

They include the areas covered by Management Responsibility and Measurement, Analyses and improvement where they are not **directly** related to either the primary or secondary processes but support them E.g: -

5.2 Quality policy
6.2 Quality objectives
9.3 Management review
9.2 Internal Audit etc

These activities are important for management to improve, control and direct the organisation and get everyone all pulling in the same direction. They often allow the auditor to see how well management understand the benefits of the ISO 9000 Family of Standards (FoS). Now termed the "Core" standards.

FINANCIAL BLACK HOLES   February 2019

A1 Example of a simple basic Car Servicing Process Map

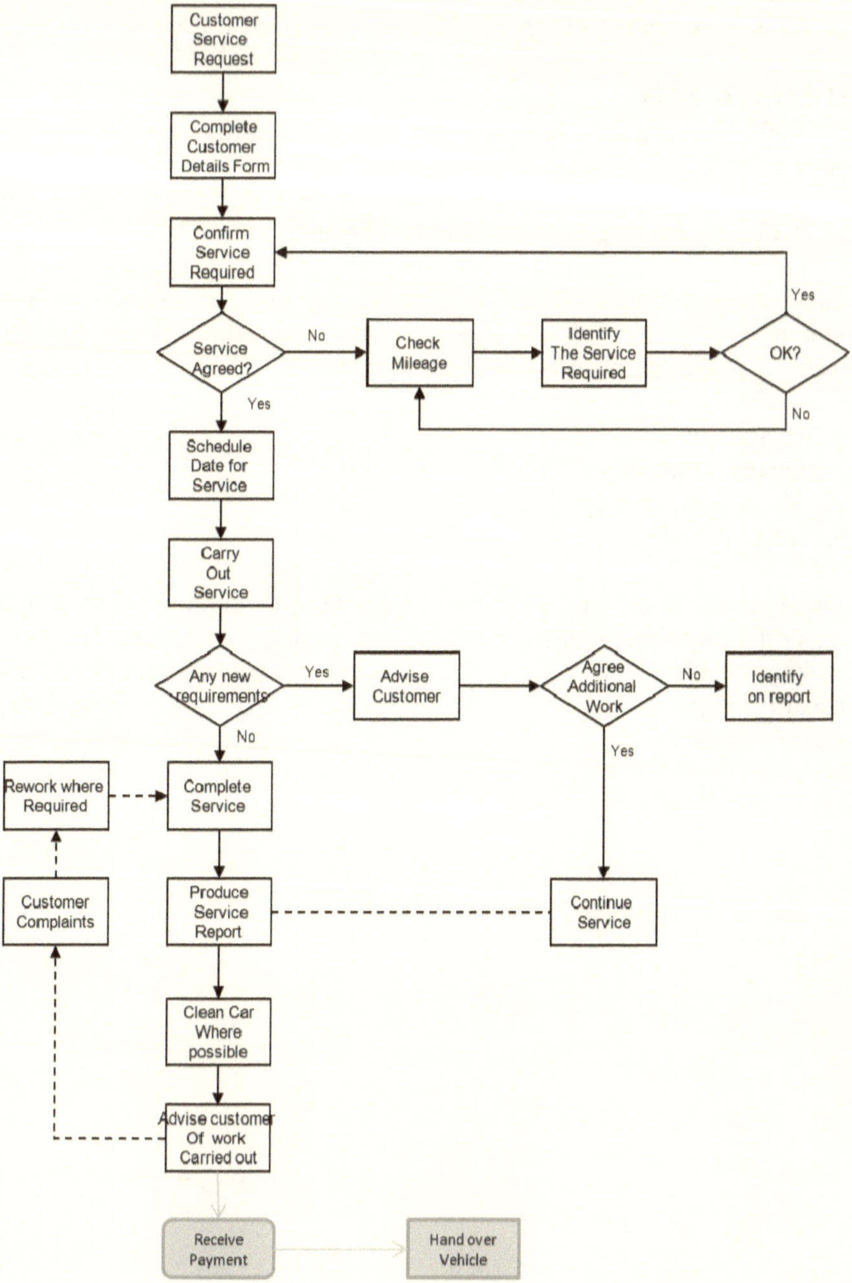

```
                    ┌──────────┐
                    │ Customer │
                    │ Service  │
                    │ Request  │
                    └────┬─────┘
                         ▼
                    ┌──────────┐
                    │ Complete │
                    │ Customer │
                    │Details Form│
                    └────┬─────┘
                         ▼
                    ┌──────────┐        ┌────────────────────────────────────────┐
                    │ Confirm  │◄───────┤                                    Yes  │
                    │ Service  │                                                  │
                    │ Required │                                             ┌────┴────┐
                    └────┬─────┘                                             │   OK?   │
                         ▼          No    ┌──────────┐   ┌──────────┐        └────┬────┘
                    ◇ Service ◇──────────►│  Check   │──►│ Identify │───────►     │ No
                    ◇ Agreed? ◇           │ Mileage  │   │The Service│             │
                         │                └──────────┘   │ Required │◄────────────┘
                       Yes                                └──────────┘
                         ▼
                    ┌──────────┐
                    │ Schedule │
                    │ Date for │
                    │ Service  │
                    └────┬─────┘
                         ▼
                    ┌──────────┐
                    │  Carry   │
                    │   Out    │
                    │ Service  │
                    └────┬─────┘
                         ▼
                    ◇ Any new ◇  Yes   ┌──────────┐      ◇  Agree  ◇  No   ┌──────────┐
                    ◇requirements◇────►│  Advise  │─────►◇Additional◇─────►│ Identify │
                         │             │ Customer │      ◇   Work   ◇      │on report │
                        No             └──────────┘           │           └──────────┘
                         ▼                                    Yes
  ┌──────────┐     ┌──────────┐                                ▼
  │Rework where│◄- -│ Complete │                          ┌──────────┐
  │ Required  │    │ Service  │                          │ Continue │
  └──────────┘     └────┬─────┘                          │ Service  │
        ▲                ▼                                └────┬─────┘
  ┌──────────┐     ┌──────────┐                                │
  │ Customer │    │ Produce  │- - - - - - - - - - - - - - - - -┘
  │Complaints│    │ Service  │
  └──────────┘     │ Report   │
        ▲          └────┬─────┘
        │                ▼
        │          ┌──────────┐
        │          │ Clean Car│
        │          │  Where   │
        │          │ possible │
        │          └────┬─────┘
        │                ▼
        │          ┌──────────┐
        └ - - - - -│Advise customer│
                   │ Of  work  │
                   │Carried out│
                   └────┬─────┘
                         ▼
                   ┌──────────┐        ┌──────────┐
                   │ Receive  │───────►│ Hand over│
                   │ Payment  │        │ Vehicle  │
                   └──────────┘        └──────────┘
```

50

FINANCIAL BLACK HOLES   February 2019

The basic car servicing flowchart will be used to demonstrate a process audit.

As already explained, the technique if you do not know the layout and departments of the organisation you are auditing, is to do a "Walk About." Following as far as is practical the primary process. During this "Walk About" notes are made of the jobs that are going through at that time including what is scheduled to go through.

It is always important to understand what drives the purchasing process. It is necessary to ensure that the contract requirements are correctly translated into the requisition. In the above case of purchasing the spares required, it is normally the requisition that defines "what is required". In the case of a main dealers car service department, it may be set up on a "Call of" basis where all the parts are well controlled with specific part numbers. Prices for parts may be controlled centrally.

It does mean that this could become critical where it is bought in from a different supplier.

NOTE: - It is important that the auditor understands the requirements of the requisition and ensures these requirements match the specification from the service contract.

If the auditor does not understand what the specification is, then the process that is being followed cannot check if the requirements of the requisition are being met.

Review what the process and activities relating to that purchasing activity are, e.g.
- What does the requisition require– does this comply with the agreed specification?
- How is the decision to purchase material made?
- How is the specification decided? Is it adequate? e.g. Special heat treated cylinder head bolts with a specified torque setting.
- Who decides what is required and do they have the authority?
- Who chooses the supplier and by what criteria?
- What is the process for bid evaluation if not call off?
- How is specification advised to the supplier?
- Are National International standards called up? Are they the latest Version?
- What controls the process?

51

 FINANCIAL BLACK HOLES   February 2019

• Are there any special packing delivery requirements? etc

These are a sample of issues that need to be followed to ensure that the right material is obtained. Many cars, even of the same model, have different specifications for the same part.

The starting point for the audit is to use the servicing of the cars and what needs to be changed, to check if the correct material has been obtained. E.g. specific oil filter, brake pads, cam belt etc. – in the above case and for simplicity-we will take just one purchase order for a cam belt. This item is crucial to the well being of the car. Cam belts have different specifications and probably part numbers so the correct item can be fitted. Then using this sample, the auditor should identify the process taken and the controls that have been applied.

Verification of Purchased Product

The next part is the receipt of the actual purchased material. It is important to check that it meets the stated requirements. The auditor should find out who does this. To what level do they inspect the item. This can take many forms and sometimes Test Certificates, Certificates of Compliance and even Declarations of Conformity, if it is a complete unit required, and if required, should be on the Purchase order. Once again the auditor will go through relevant purchase orders related to parts required for the sample of cars chosen. Again all these requirements should be clearly defined in the Purchase Order. Auditors should always read the Purchase Orders to ensure they are adequate and what has been called up is clear and unambiguous. The final check is probably against the Goods Inwards procedure as there may be special tests to be carried out on receipt. This may also include storage and preservation requirements. There is no point storing material incorrectly thus making it unusable. It is not unusual for personnel, in their ignorance, to open packaging and destroy the preservation that had been called up in the Purchase Order. There is sometimes a specific need to ensure that spares are used on a "First In First Out" basis (FIFO) to ensure that the oldest material is not left unused for longer than necessary. This is especially important for material that has a shelf life.

Throughout the audit process, it is vital that the samples are LINKED and from the same TRAIL. If the same trail is not followed it is not possible to comply with the scope of ISO 9001.

FINANCIAL BLACK HOLES   February 2019

9.0 - LEADERSHIP

Leadership is intended to cover the people who are successful or advanced in a particular role. They range from managers, owners directors, chief executives, and many others. What does this mean? In the revised ISO 9001 2015, it can simply be stated as taking accountability for how effective the organisation is.

LEADERSHIP

PERSONNEL RESPONSIBLE AND ACCOUNTABLE FOR HOW EFFECTIVE AND EFFICIENT AN ORGANISATION IS

Not advancing into too much detail regarding all the aspects of leadership, the intention in this book is to highlight where activities are ineffective. This would allow organisations to reduce "Chronic Waste". Leaders should have relevant knowledge of the specific product and service the organisation provides. It requires those who are in a Leadership role's to obtain "Information" on how the organisation performs. Again referring to the ISO standards Information = Meaningful Data. This term has come up time and time again in this book. If what is provided to Leadership is not accurate information, then there is no chance to know if what is taking place is effective.

INFORMATION = MEANINGFUL DATA

The revised ISO 9001:2015 is considered by some to be a major change however the scope of ISO 9001 has not changed. It still specifies the requirements for a management system where an organisation needs to demonstrate its ability to consistently provide products and services that meet customer and applicable statutory and regulatory requirements. This means that the standard has a restrictive scope primarily aimed at consistently meeting the customer requirements.

The revision has now included the clause "Context of an organisation". This is intended to encourage organisations to look beyond the system they control and take into account other organisations that can impact on their ability to meet customer requirements.

53

 FINANCIAL BLACK HOLES   February 2019

The statutory and regulatory requirements are only those that apply to the products and services the organisation provides to their customers.

A number of clauses directly related to Leadership will now be highlighted:

Clause 4 Context of an organisation

Covers the context in which the organisation operates and the interested parties that could affect their ability to meet the requirements of the standard. It includes external as well as internal issues as it relates to the scope.

Clause 4.3 requires the organisation to determine its own scope by defining where the boundaries are set for the organisations management system. In other words, what is inside and what is outside the defined boundaries, as they relate to the scope of that particular organisation. Clause 4.4 covers the resultant quality management system needed to achieve the scope of that standard.

This clause 4.3 in the ISO 9001:2015 will allow each organisation to look at what, how and when the new terms such as Risk, Opportunities and Interested parties that could affect the organisations ability to consistently meet customer requirements. In doing this the organisation can adjust the scope 4.3 so it is specific to their business.

54

FINANCIAL BLACK HOLES   February 2019

THE SPIRAL OF SCOPE (HOPE!)

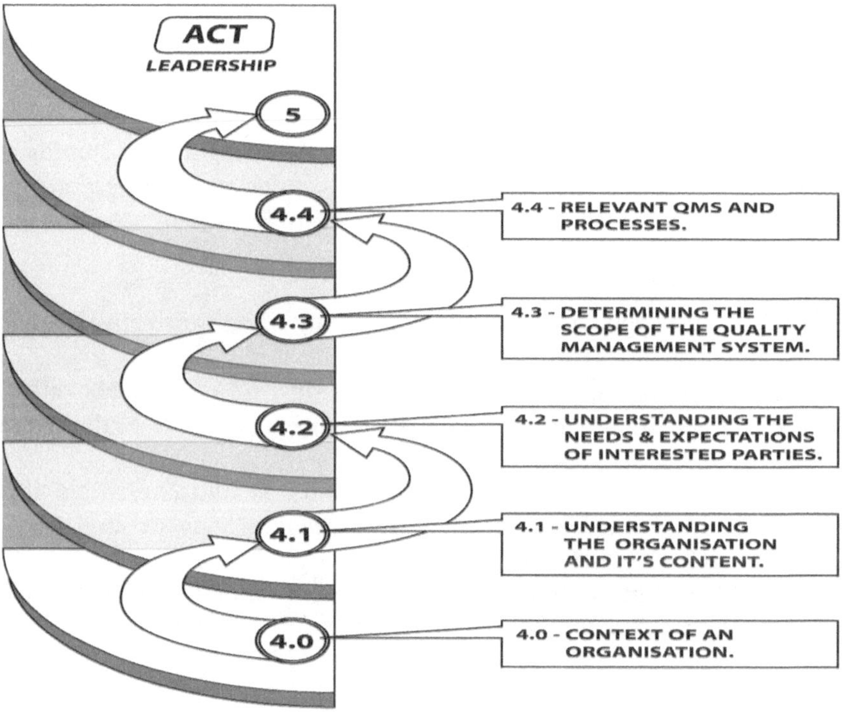

ACT
LEADERSHIP

5

4.4 — 4.4 - RELEVANT QMS AND PROCESSES.

4.3 — 4.3 - DETERMINING THE SCOPE OF THE QUALITY MANAGEMENT SYSTEM.

4.2 — 4.2 - UNDERSTANDING THE NEEDS & EXPECTATIONS OF INTERESTED PARTIES.

4.1 — 4.1 - UNDERSTANDING THE ORGANISATION AND IT'S CONTENT.

4.0 — 4.0 - CONTEXT OF AN ORGANISATION.

©2015 PDQMS

It makes sense to go through this logical sequence from 4.1 through to 4.4 to understand what Leadership have to deal with in the new ISO 9001:2015 standard

Clause 5 Leadership
Has an emphasis on leadership not just management.
- Top management has to show a demonstrated involvement in the management system
- The policy has to be made available to all parties and communicated to interested parties
First glance this seems the same as what has gone before namely policy, organisational roles, responsibilities and authorities, communication etc
- The main difference is that top management has to have a "hands on" involvement and be able to **demonstrate** their commitment to the management system. (See Spiral of Scope)

 FINANCIAL BLACK HOLES   February 2019

Clause 9 Performance evaluation

Having carried out the activities within clause 8 operation it is time to check the performance.

- It covers what, how and when things are monitored, measured, analysed and evaluated
- It includes audits, management reviews which should include deciding on what action should be taken to prevent problems recurring, or stop them happening in the first place. (Risk!) If a discipline needs procedures or other documents they can be added as required by the organisation

Clause 10 Improvement

This is where you address non conformity and corrective action recognising that

- "Risk and Opportunity" is intended to, not only address the above but, **prevent things happening (Taking over from Preventative Action from ISO 9001:2008)**
- There is no mention of procedures and work instructions within ISO 9001 2015. Relevant documents such as procedures may be used where they are seen to be beneficial
- The need to continually improve is a basic premise for all standards using the new common structure of clauses introduced in Annex SL

<u>SUMMARY</u>

It should be noted that Leadership would benefit from being aware of all clauses within the ISO 9001 2015, however the above is a small sample of relevant issues from ISO 9001:2015 that directly impact on improvement. ISO standards are now using the Annex SL common clause structure that will allow easy integration of certifiable standards. (e.g. Quality Environmental and Health and Safety). The use of the Annex SL approach is to make it easier for organisations that wish to be certified to more than one standard, to introduce an integrated system.

This requires the organisation to look at the scope of each standard and see what issues affect its business. The organisation then needs to ensure they know what these issues are, how to manage them including, where appropriate, the relevant interested parties, even those that are outside their direct control that could affect their ability to achieve the intended output taking into account the scope. The quality management system is the responsibility of the organisation and there is no attempt to impose requirements on them, as long as the organisation can demonstrate they have thought about and dealt with all relevant issues. Leadership is a key

FINANCIAL BLACK HOLES   February 2019

issue for success. It highlights the importance of planning the management system to ensure it is effective. It covers all the supporting issues that can influence the success or failure of their activities. This leads to the actual operation, planning and control etc. which is termed Operation Clause 8 in ISO 9001:2015. It then concludes with an evaluation of the performance that has taken place, identifying areas that need improvement.

The two major changes within Annex SL are the importance of "Leadership" clause 5 and how Management responsibility needs to deal with Clause 4 "Context of an organisation".

One area where there is some misunderstanding is the Quality Policy 3.5.9 It is important that organisations ensure that all personnel understand what the quality policy means. In fact it is an important tool to get everyone in the organisation to pull in the same direction.

It covers having quality objectives. These objectives are not about just the quality system but about anything that can impact on the product or service provided to the customer. Objectives should be measurable and consistent with the quality policy. The term SMART is often used to help people understand: -

S Specific   Clearly define what the objective is with a clear problem statement
M Measurable That the objective is measurable
A Achievable   There is no point having an objective that you can't achieve
R Realistic   It must be realistic in that it is something that can be solved
T Timely   It must be something with a sensible time scale

An early formally recognised improvement project that Shell Expro Aberdeen carried out included off shore Casing, where the objective was to prevent the number of leaks that were occurring. The initial timescale was 6 months. Within the 6 month time scale leaks had been stopped however it took 3 years before the objective was fully closed down and even then one of the measurable issues could not be resolved. After three years there was to be an award for "Holding the Gains". Two weeks before the award ceremony in Aberdeen was to take place there was a leak!!

The cause of the leak was resolved in days when the facilitator on the improvement project, based in Aberdeen, went through all the matric flow charts that had been produced and identified what had taken place. He quickly identified the cause of the leak. The process had been

57

FINANCIAL BLACK HOLES   February 2019

compromised by allowing a damaged casing to be sent ashore for repair. The repair was carried out using a machine shop that could not achieve the accuracy.

Leadership Responsibility, authority and communication (5.0) is always a difficult issue as it is not easy to keep everyone informed. ISO 9001 requires that someone from the management team must take responsibility for quality.

This then leads to management review (9.3) and although this is important in some instances it has lost credibility and is not seen to add much value. This is evidenced by the management review being annual. If something as important as quality is only looked at once per year, it shows how little credibility quality has within the organisation. In fact, many organisations will freely state they only carry out management review because they have to, as it is a requirement in the ISO 9001 standard. The whole purpose of a Management Review is to allow the organisation to gather "information" from audits, customers, processes and product conformity, corrective and preventive action follow up on previous management reviews and from that information identify activities for improvement.

INFORMATION = MEANINGFUL DATA
ISO 9000:2015

Some management review minutes indicate that there has been little benefit from the meeting. In fact it seems as if having the meeting is the objective. Even when an action activity is identified there is often no time scale defined. It is this failure to agree a specific time frame for completion of the action that undermines the credibility of the process. In many instances staff have to carry on with their own jobs and action parties have their name followed by ASAP or Ongoing. If these audits are annual, as often happens with Certification Audits, it is no wonder little improvement is being achieved. Where an action party is identified it is essential a realistic time frame and actual date is identified. If this does not occur it can undermine quality as they are too often accepted by certification bodies on the grounds that a management reviews has taken place. The review output is often not well managed especially the resources need to achieve the improvement.

FINANCIAL BLACK HOLES   February 2019

9.1 Management Review

This is one area where the organisations leadership must be provided with information.

INFORMATION = MEANINGFUL DATA
ISO 9000:2015

The above definition is one of the shortest in the ISO 9000 Fundamentals and Vocabulary standard. As simple as the definition for information is, it is very often not recognised when what is provided is just data.

Example
Is the following information?
In 2010 there were 20 internal audits carried out and 60 nonconformities were raised.
In 2011 there were 20 internal audits carried out and 40 nonconformities were raised
In 2012 there were 20 internal audits carried out and 20 nonconformities were raised

Many students indicate that this is information. The data provided does apparently show a trend which is, on the surface, useful. However, what is provided gives no information on what was actually found within those non conformities. The reason being it does not actually tell the reader anything other than the number of nonconformities has been reduced. It is not possible from this to decide what if anything needs to be done as it is just raw data.

The whole purpose of a management review meeting is to make decision on what is working well and what is not. How should the internal audits be presented? To make this more effective it would be necessary to break the data down into a format that does give information.
e.g.
* How many nonconformities affected the organisations ability to provide the customer the correct product/service?
* How many of them were because procedures or instructions were not being followed?
* How many were because of poorly maintained equipment?

FINANCIAL BLACK HOLES   February 2019

* How many were because testing or measuring equipment was not correct?
* How many were because of operator error?

It is not possible to give a definitive list of concerns because it needs to be based on what the nonconformities were about. This means that each nonconformity should be looked at to see how best to clearly define the type of problem and its impact on the business.

When this is done it gives an opportunity for management to decide what improvements should be made. However, from experience too many management reviews are carried out to comply with ISO 9001 and even the organisations management do not believe what takes place is useful. When they are asked what the purpose is they say it is to comply with ISO 9001 and retain their certification.

This brings to mind one of many instances of concern.

When a management review audit was carried out it was noted that the management had little or no information to make any decisions. The CEO was advised that the management review was not effective.

The CEO answer was: -
"Where does it state, in ISO 9001, that the management review has to be effective? All it states is that a management review has to be carried out by considering a list of bullet points and then develop the management review outputs and we have done that and noted the action that needs to be taken".

It is this drive to comply with what the standard states rather than ascertain what would actually benefit the business that undermines management systems. Is it important to gather information where things have gone wrong and take action to prevent them happening again? I can only hope that this requirement is just common sense yet from what has already been stated in previous chapters there is a failure to recognise what corrective action is.

FINANCIAL BLACK HOLES   February 2019

From the CEO response there is little chance of taking corrective action as the material provided for the management review gives little or no real information.

Another classic failure of the Management Review is where an action party has been identified yet this is followed by "As Soon as Possible" (ASAP) or "Ongoing". **One amusing response when after the three management review meetings were examined the same ASAP problem had not been closed out.** The action party, let us say Mr Smith, was asked why this action had not been completed his response was **it was not possible!**

When this is mentioned to students in a training session they often indicate that this is how they do things in their company so it is little wonder that improvement is difficult to achieve.

What should occur is that the action party should be asked to provide a time frame for how long this action would take. Leaving open ended time frames such as ASAP and Ongoing achieves little or nothing. The reason for obtaining a time frame is if the person cannot action this in a reasonable time it might be better to appoint someone else to do that specific job.

Quality improvement is an information intensive activity that should be broken down in order that it highlights what can be done. It is not unusual to have to gather more information and one method of sorting this is to present the problems in the terms of the "Cost of Nonconformity" often simplified to CONC. This is because if the overall cost of each specific problem is identified it can then help decide what should be tackled first. This chapter was just to highlight how in too many cases management reviews are only carried out because a standard requires it not because the activity can be seen as a benefit to the business.

 FINANCIAL BLACK HOLES   February 2019

10.0 - IMPROVEMENT REGARDING THE EXAMPLES

This section takes a look at what should have been done with the examples in section 4 and 5, where there was no recognition that what had taken place was ineffective.

10.1 Review of complaints

As already explained, this covers a review of the complaint process where the person carrying out the review was restricted by the scope that indicated that they could not look at any actual complaints. In fact, they were only allowed to look at the seven documents given to them by the organisation. From the Competence Model (Attachement C) it is either **Unconscious incompetence**, where the individual does not know how a review should be carried out or it is a deliberate ploy to defend what the organisation has done regarding the complaints they have received.

What should be done?

This is where the difficulty occurs if this is what they have been taught and they do not recognise that anything is wrong then it is difficult to take any "Correction" or "Corrective Action" especially as more senior personnel cannot see that what took place was ineffective.

Major Concern

It is worth noting that the organisation in question actually trains people in this type of activity. This is why personnel trained by this particular organisation feel unable to challenge what they have been taught even if they recognise it is illogical.

It is the same as the so called "System Audit" where auditors only audit the documented system. In fact many believe you cannot audit without a procedure. Just auditing the documented system is not effective. What should occur is a "Process Audit" where the auditor takes the time to understand what the output from the process should be then using that information checks to see if what is taking place, including the competence of the personnel within the organisation, can consistently achieve the desired output.

FINANCIAL BLACK HOLES   February 2019

10.2 Council Hedge Inspection

This activity had so many issues that were incorrect that is worth mentioning some of them: -

1. The Council refused to give a complaint number at the beginning because they indicated the complainant had appointed a legal representative.

Concern - Why would an organisation not register each complaint?

2. When this was found to be incorrect they still refused to give a complaint number as it had then been passed to another government department for review

Concern - Again the system still stopped them logging a complaint and it seems as soon as some other department takes over they have no interest

3. The department who were doing the review could not locate the documents and they had to be emailed to them as they indicated that this occurred on a number of occasions and they were very busy

Concern - It stated that misplacing documents or documents not getting through to the correct section was not unusual as they were so busy. Could identifying why there are so many complaints be an opportunity to improve?

4. The reviewing department indicated that there was a case to answer

Agreement - there was a justification to review the process.

5. When the Review body was asked what the review consisted of, they stated they were not allowed to check if the Councils processes were effective. They just checked if the council had followed their procedures. It was pointed out that the complaint was that there procedures were ineffective. The review body then stated it was not their job to see if what the Council did was effective or efficient.

Concern - From what was stated they are not responsible for checking if what takes place was effective

63

 FINANCIAL BLACK HOLES   February 2019

6.   The Review was then cancelled by the complainant as the action proposed by that reviewing body would not have been able to see if the Councils process was effective.

Concern - The complaint was about how ineffective the councils process was yet to this point no one was responsible for ascertain if the process was effective

7.   This brought the complaint back to the Council who then gave it a complaint number

Concern - The council have now registered the complaint but do they have all the information on the complaint up to this point? It is unlikely.

8.   The Council then reviewed the complaint and indicated that there was nothing wrong as they had followed the Councils system.

Concern - Once again they indicate they have followed their system

9.   This was then taken to the Ombudsman who also stated he would not investigate. He did not believe it was necessary because the Complainant had not suffered any significant disadvantage

Concern - So the complainant had suffered some disadvantage, but not enough to investigate

10. The Ombudsman was asked had he read the Inspection Report and the answer was no.

Concern - How can the Ombudsman respond on a complaint about the Inspection report when he has not read it?

11. This was then taken up with the local MP who was asked how can a "Local Council" be challenged over the system they use when no one wishes to review it to see if what had taken place is effective and could be justified?

Agreement -The local MP accepted that there was a question that needed to be answered

12. The Local MP then made contact with the senior personnel at the Council and it was arranged that the Executive Director of the Council would get involved.

FINANCIAL BLACK HOLES   February 2019

Concern - The Executive was advised of the concern about the effectiveness of the councils system

13. The Director then rejected the complaint as the Council had followed their system

Concern – Does blindly following the system overrule common sense?

14. The complainant then asked the Executive Director two questions the second one was: - Should the BRE guidance document be used to penalise owners of larger gardens? **The answer given categorically stated that it is not the intention to penalise owners of larger gardens.**

Concern – This should indicate that what took place was wrong but this was ignored?

15. The Executive Director was asked why the height of the hedge had been increased above the 4 meters accepted for privacy. Neither he, nor anyone else in the council would answer this question.

Concern - Once again no one would even consider that their system might need improvement

16. Finally the Executive Director indicated his staff had spent too much time on this and he would no longer respond to any questions.

Concern – If you cannot answer the question refuse to respond to any further correspondence.

The above is a short summary of a long journey and is indicative of how an organisation, such as a Council where their income is secured by government, can ignore any complaints as there appears to be no one within their system responsible for judging if the process is effective. There were around 12 people involved and the estimated cost for just dealing with this one complaint to the council would be around 8 man days at say £ 400/day? Estimated 8 x £ 400 = £ 3,200. This is Chronic Waste as there is no incentive to investigate their system.

So how does anybody deal with an Organisation such as the Council when there is no alternative and all those involved see that there is nothing wrong with their system how can this be progressed?

FINANCIAL BLACK HOLES   February 2019

The interesting thing is, that because councils use a government approved guidance document they hide behind it. A simple justification for the council response was illustrated when the council were asked why their Inspection report did not have a clause numbering system to enable anyone to cross refer a concern to the Inspection clause number the Council stated: -

"The Government does not require us to number the clauses".

This shows there is no consideration given to the benefit this would be to the customer.

If the body that does the "Reviews" of complaints are very busy and even misplace or lose documents and things do not get to the right location, would it not be useful to attempt to reduce the number of complaints?

This is similar as the previous "Complaints Review" as it can only be considered to be **Unconscious incompetence**, fed by the fact that they do not have anyone that can do anything about it as there is no accountability because they refer to Government approved documents.

Conclusion

The Council and all other parties in the process hide behind their system. There are so many different parties that are involved when throughout the process that there is no one responsible or accountable for what takes place. The personnel within all those department have their income assured, unlike any private sector organisation that obtains their income from paying customers if they fail to meet customer expectations the customers cannot go elsewhere. It is not possible to improve as demonstrated by the responses from all involved because despite repeated requests to answer a simple question of: -

WHAT JUSTIFICATION HAVE THE COUNCIL GOT TO INCREASE THE HEIGHT OF THE HEDGE ABOVE THE 4 METERS REQUIRED FOR PRIVACY?

The council and all other departments involved, including the Ombudsman, would not respond except to state they followed government guidelines.

The only conclusion to be made is that there is no justification. In fact even the Ombudsman investigating the complaint stated that if the council

FINANCIAL BLACK HOLES   February 2019

used a government approved document no Ombudsman would accept that what had been done was wrong. There was no recognition of it being a **guidance document**. The only conclusion would be that this was because of **Unconscious incompetence.**

There is still nothing that can be done unless the reviewing body has a change in its responsibility and authorities and there is someone made accountable. This responsible party would gather all the information about how many complaints have been made across all councils to see, how many complaints have been received on hedges? This individual or body accountable for investigating chronic waste should then identify the costs of dealing with these complaints. (Cost of Nonconformity)

If information is obtained it would mean that there would be objective evidence obtained from the root cause/s to allow appropriate action to be taken to improve the process by stopping or reducing the instances of it happening again.

A simple approach would be to ensure all decisions can be justified.

The above examples are likely to increase the chronic waste rather than improve unless effective "Corrective Action" is taken.

FINANCIAL BLACK HOLES   February 2019

10.3 Grenfell Tower Fire

This is more difficult to deal with, as it is still part of an enquiry so it is not possible to say anything other than what has already been mentioned. That scope of the enquiry was too wide and as stated by the legal representative in charge of the enquiry, "It is unlikely to satisfy those parties affected by the fire"

I will leave the reader to decide if this is **Unconscious incompetence** or something else?

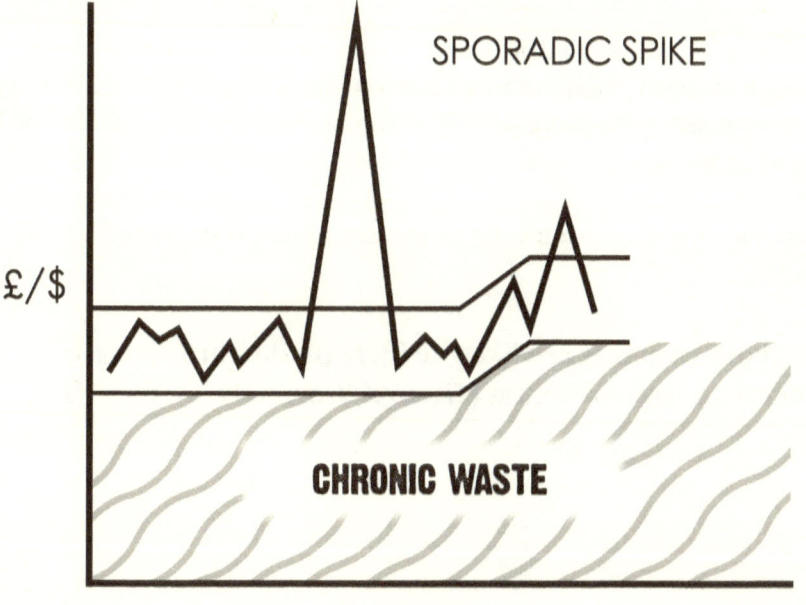

This diagram shows the chronic waste increasing when it is not recognised that what is being done is ineffective. The only way is up! In other words more Chronic Waste.

FINANCIAL BLACK HOLES   February 2019

The following situations from section 5 of this book where the organisation recognize they have not provided an effective service. This is positive, however, in many cases they have failed to prevent the same thing happening again.

10.4 Organisations that recognised that their processes were ineffective.

It has not been possible to ascertain whether they just carried out "Correction" by taking action to satisfy the customer, or take the time to identify the "Root Cause" of the problem and do something that would stop it occurring again. (Corrective Action). Although some examples did indicate that they had not taken corrective action. This was because the organisation involved was still offering the service despite being advised that they should not.

Chapter 4 Overall Conclusion

The reliance of organisations to defer to their system and defend any complaints is of concern.

The response received is that they have followed their system. This mainly occurs where there is no issue over the financial income of the organisation, as income is assured by government.

Even where common sense would indicate that just looking at an organisations documented system would give no information on how effective the processes are.

In fact it is not possible to even know if the documented system was even being followed never mind if it was effective.

There are some instances where the scope is modified to ensure that an effective review or enquiry cannot take place.

There is also evidence where a Government approved Guidance document is used as if it is a requirement. This is an example where the organisation hides behind their system

Chapter 5 Overall conclusions

This covers organisation that do recognise that what has taken place is wrong.

 FINANCIAL BLACK HOLES   February 2019

The problem here is that in too many cases only **"Correction" (Action to eliminate a detected non conformity)** takes place. In other words the organisation makes things right.

The opportunity to find the root cause and take **"Corrective Action" (Action to eliminate the cause of the nonconformity to prevent recurrence)** is ignored

These terms are clearly defined in ISO 9000:2015 Fundamentals and Vocabulary.

The failure to take effective action allows the problem to reoccur causing "Chronic Waste".

In some instances it's because they do not realise that what they are doing is ineffective. The other situation is where they recognise that what they do is wrong but only satisfy the customer by correcting the error. This can be done by paying compensation and/or spending a lot of time dealing with the problem but not resolving it. All of which supports chronic waste.

QUESTION TO ALL READERS
What does your organisation do?

All the book is trying to achieve is encourage organisations to identify which of the above approaches their organisation takes?

Do you gather information on all the things that go wrong? Is this actually information?

Is anything being done to improve what takes place?

FINANCIAL BLACK HOLES   February 2019

11.0 - GENERAL IMPROVEMENT

Not all organisations use the Plan, Do, Check, Act approach yet when you look at how beneficial it can be to the business, it makes sense to implement it.

All organisations have to apply the "Plan and Do" approach and ISO 9001 covers this quite effectively as it encourages a clear understanding of what the customer wants and asks the organisation to be sure they have the resources and skills to be able to achieve that requirement. Within ISO 9001 it also asks them to plan how it will be carried out.

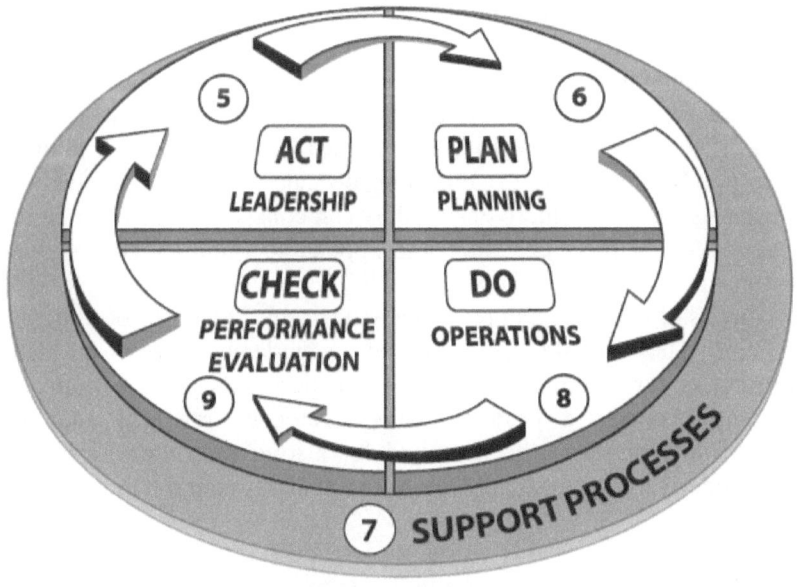

Some organisations miss out as they don't gather information about the problems they have experienced. In fact they see it as being of no interest once the problem has been **corrected** they just move onto the next job. This misses out on the opportunity to take **corrective action** where the cause of the problem is identified and effort made to prevent it happening again. Corrective action is intended to prevent money being wasted by stopping the problem happening again. In fact in many cases it is this waste that reduces the profitability of the business.

 FINANCIAL BLACK HOLES   February 2019

It is worth once again mentioning the misunderstood terms used in ISO 9000:2015.

From **ISO 9000:2015** they are: -

Correction 3.12.3
Action to eliminate a detected non conformity.

Corrective Action 3.12.2
Action to eliminate the causes of a nonconformity and to prevent recurrance

Preventive Action 3.12.1
Action to eliminate the cause of a **potential** nonconformity or other **potential** undesirable situation

Note: - ISO 9001:2008 the previous version required a procedure for Preventive Action and Corrective Action. However, there are no longer any specific procedures specified in the latest ISO 9001:2015. The drive is for the Leadership of the organisation to decide what is required within their management system, to ensure they can consistently provide products and services that meet customer and applicable statutory and regulatory requirements. (See ISO 9001 Scope). This approach makes sense provided the organisations leadership understand why these procedures are beneficial. They enable all personnel to understand how to identify opportunities for improvement and where necessary, take action before something becomes a problem. This cannot be repeated enough as although the terms have been around for a long time the terms are not always understood because they are were not always taught.

Correction is simple in that you just correct the error and that is allowed in ISO 9001. However, it also requires you to carry out **Corrective Action** which means finding out the cause of the problem and doing something to stop it happening again.

Where the biggest confusion occurs is with **Preventive Action** as too many quality professionals do not understand that if a problem has already occurred, then although you are being asked to prevent it occurring again that is NOT the meaning of **Preventive Action,** as defined in the previous version of ISO 9000:2005. I was advised that Preventive action has been removed from ISO 9000:2015 because it is not understood.

FINANCIAL BLACK HOLES   February 2019

Why wasn't it taught properly?

"Preventive Action" is quite clear if you actually read the definitions in ISO 9000:2015. **Preventive action** uses the term **"potential"** twice (see above) **Corrective Action** states **"detected"**. Therefore if some nonconformity has already been detected, it is not covered by "Preventive Action".

Preventive Action is only applicable **BEFORE** a problem has occurred.

It has been stated that preventive action has been replaced with the term "Risk based thinking" although the definition for Preventive action 3.12.1 is still included in ISO 9000:2015 and "Risk based thinking" is not.

The importance of ISO 9000 is quite clear if you recognize that the Normative reference clause in both ISO 9001:2008 and the new ISO 9001 2015 states that ISO 9000 is indispensable to the application of ISO 9001:2015. That is why I have on many occasions, indicated that they are a **"Matched pair"** of standards even though this statement is disputed by many quality professionals. This is not surprising when not all of ISO 9001 is taught.

As this book is also aimed at smaller to medium size businesses, we will use a simple logical approach without complex methodology and terminology.

A technique I have used is the "Problem sheet". This is a simple A4 page similar to a Non Conformity Report that just captures information on problems (Attachment E). This attachment is just an example and it is a good idea for organisations to develop their own version. It is recommended that there is an opportunity to include the Cost of Non Conformity (CONC) This is where a simple quick rough estimate is made over how much it has cost the organisation to carry out the correction. It should include the cost of any material that has to be obtained, the work needed to make the item or repair it as well as the cost of the time spent dealing with this. To make the "Problem Sheet" stand out, it is recommended that a coloured A4 paper is used and made readily available to all staff.

The "Problem Sheet" should include the date, location and the person who filled it in.

 FINANCIAL BLACK HOLES   February 2019

The person who completes it can remain nameless if being anonymous helps get problem sheets completed. It then has a space for the staff member or other to fill in what the problem was and if possible, what impact it had on the job. As already mentioned the problem sheet should include what it has cost (CONC). On completion this is then handed in to management or a nominated responsible party.

This approach was used to capture defects over a specific Shut Down. It was advised that no one would fill them in. It was written in English on one side and the local language on the other using the same format both sides.

During a 4 week shut down over 100 Problem Sheets on light yellow paper were filled in. After analyses, a direct loss of £250,000 plus an extra week added to the shutdown gave the information that could be dealt with. The above price loss does not covered the cost of not having the equipment working for a further week, that was around £ 0.5 Million. This waste was investigated and it was identified that ten of the problems caused a potential loss of £200,000.

This fitted well with the old 80/20 rule regarding the costing and met the principle of a small number of problems causing a large loss of both time and money.

Having this information allowed these issues to be prioritised using Pareto analyses and time was spent on Corrective Action on these 10 problem areas. Other problems were also identified and some actioned, although the 10 problems were the priority.

This was just one improvement process on a shutdown project which paid off as the next project was carried out on time and the losses were reduced to less than £ 75,000. (To those doing the maths new problems occurred.) However the latest project 1 year later benefited with a reduced time frame and smaller losses.

It was also identified that the most significant problem, that had caused the most losses, had occurred at least twice before and NO "Corrective Action" had taken place only "Correction".

These annual shut downs took place on a regular 5 year frequency covering the five similar units. (One shut down per year) In fact the time

FINANCIAL BLACK HOLES   February 2019

taken on each shut down was reduced because of this and other changes that took place having gathered accurate information ("Meaningful Data").

The first thing to do, as already stated, is to identify the problem

PROBLEMS

This leads us back to the beginning of problem solving.

It is essential that a problem statement is written. This can then be part of the Quality Objectives that are set for the organisation. It does of course need the problem to be identified hence the use of "Problem" sheets as they identify what the concern is.

So it is necessary to decide what an effective problem statement is, and what is not.

Problem statements should only define the problem. **A very simple example follows** to illustrate how this works.

PROBLEM STATEMENT

E.g. we have many instances where fitters are going out to the customer without all the equipment and tools they need to carry out the task. This causes many man-hours to be lost as they have to return to the workshop or retail outlets to obtain the material required.

A method of checking if the problem statement is good is to score it against the following four elements: -

a) Is it a simple statement
b) Are numbers (Figures) provided
c) Is any background knowledge given
d) Are any costs given

The scoring is simple. Just like any good system you score each element of the problem statement so if the problem statement is good it would score 10.

To keep it simple we can score each of the four elements at 2.5 marks each.

Note: - you can weigh the scoring if you wish. (Say 4 marks for cost)

FINANCIAL BLACK HOLES   February 2019

This is a simple method to judge if the above "Problem Statement" is good.

REMEMBER THIS IS REALLY JUST A BEST GUESS
Using the KIS approach (Keep it simple) let us look at the problem statement

a)   Is it a simple statement?
Yes it is simple and does give a picture of the problem
Score 2.0

b)   Are numbers provided?
This could be the number of times this occurs and currently there are no numbers provided
Score 0

c)   Is any background knowledge given
Yes it covers outside work however there may be other activities where this takes place
Score 1.5 or 2.0

d)   Are any costs given?
No there are no costs or information about how much this is costing
Score 0

TOTAL SCORE
4 out of 10 so it is not such a good problem statement

What other "Meaningful Data" would help?
You could mind map this and see what comes up, however for the purpose of the book we will add the types of things that would improve the problem statement.

Point b) Are numbers provided? What would you like to see?
For example over the last month there were 25 outside jobs carried out, 12 of them required people to leave the job site and spend time away gathering material.

Seems useful however which month are we talking about as that would make it objective. Would it be useful to also identify the number of man hours required to tackle the 25 outside jobs? What percentage of time is being lost? Hopefully you get the picture

76

FINANCIAL BLACK HOLES   February 2019

Point d) Are any costs given? What would we like to see?
Assuming that the man-hours spent away from the workplace gathering material added up to 12 hours over the month in question. Seems useful but what percentage of the total man-hours for outside work does this cover?

Again good data but what is it actually costing in pounds? Should we use an average hourly cost of £50. Total cost £ 600. Should this be gathered over a few months?

Hopefully you can see what would help.

So let's rewrite the problem statement

REVISED PROBLEM STATEMENT
We have many instances where fitters are going out to the customer without all the equipment and tools they need to carry out the task. This has caused 12 man-hours to be lost costing £ 600 in July alone as they have to return to the workshop or retail outlets to obtain the material. Therefore customer complaints happen regarding the delay. In some cases, resulting in having to return the following day to finish the job.

This is not a perfect problem statement. However it is a little bit better than before, as it does give some level of information, therefore would allow the problem to be investigated.

We still don't know if this is across just two crews of two people or twenty crews of two people so there is still a lot of information needed. It is however better than the first problem statement.

An interesting fact is no support will be given unless the costs are put in money terms.

In fact many quality managers use the "Cost of Non-Conformity" termed (CONC). As this can often make managers sit up when they see the cost in £'s (CONC) and it then gets a reaction. The downside is all organisations have what "Juran" calls Chronic Waste. This simply means waste that goes on and on for ever as everyone ignores it. This is often where only "Correction" takes place not "Corrective Action" and is where the same problem reoccurs on a regular basis. This is often what is considered a small cost per incident but when it continues for years it adds up. That is

FINANCIAL BLACK HOLES   February 2019

why ISO 9001 is so keen on "Corrective Action" to remove this chronic waste. Even today many ISO 9001 Certified organisations only carry out "correction".

This is only a brief introduction and awareness of the benefits that could be obtained if the management system was set up to capture this information. Too many times people say they do not have the time to do this. This brings in the following statement

I DON'T HAVE ENOUGH TIME
TO DO THIS PROPERLY
AS I AM TOO BUSY CORRECTING
EARLIER MISTAKES

As you can see, this is just a basic introduction but when your organisation automatically gathers information on where time and money are being lost, it is not difficult to take action to remove these losses. It is not necessary to take action straight away just gather information.

To all those quality professionals who may wish to ridicule this simplistic approach. I will say it is aimed at keeping it simple to allow the process to be understood and applied by anyone.

Many businesses miss out on improvement as they feel it takes too long and is too complicated. Well it does not take a lot of time and it is not complicated. In fact it takes minutes to fill in a problem sheet and when they are evaluated, say every quarter or year, it can give sound objective information. It is not even necessary to take action over every problem found; all it does it give the organisation a choice. Simple common sense will let you decide if it is worth taking "corrective action". In some cases, it will not but you decide if it would benefit the business.

I would suggest this approach is tried. This was applied in a country where I was advised it would not work and I can assure you it did. Hopefully a few organisations will use this approach and if they do they will benefit by having sound information that they can work with to help them improve.

The most amusing problem reported was that one of the engineers damaged his safety shoes and because his feet were large (Size 13) there was no spare available. He was not allowed on site and his role was crucial and even flying the shoes in from Singapore meant a day was lost.

78

FINANCIAL BLACK HOLES   February 2019

JOHN RUSKIN

The common law of business prohibits paying a little and getting a lot. It can't be done. If you deal with the lowest bidder its well to add something for the risk you run and if you do that you will have enough to pay for something better

John Ruskin – 1819 - 1900

 FINANCIAL BLACK HOLES   February 2019

12.0 - HOW TO LOOK FOR OPPORTUNITIES TO IMPROVE?

Let us look at the sources of information: -

- **Complaints** Are opportunities to improve
- **Audits** Are ineffective if they are just auditing the documented system
- **Management reviews** Where information is examined and decisions made
- **Logging "Correction"** that has taken place and the impact on the business
- **Analysing how effective "Corrective Action"** has been at removing the problem
- **Recording Preventative action** and its benefits and effectiveness
- **Develop Problem sheets (Attachment E)** identify and recording problems
- **Review all Problems (Attachment E)** obtaining information and analyse
- **Customer feedback** and whether they are satisfied or not
- **Monitoring and measuring** the effectiveness of processes
- **Monitoring and measuring the product**
- **Controlling non-conforming product** and investigating the cause
- **Analyses of the "meaningful" data**
- **Management reviews** where decisions can be made.

The above has been used for decades by effective managers, however, far too often, management reviews are given just "Raw" data that may indicate trends but does not provide information in a manner that can allow the organisation to take action and improve. The intention in this book has been to concentrate on two types of complaint using three examples of each. The book has concentrated on the first three sources of information above. Complaints, (See section 4 and 5) Audits and how some audits are ineffective as they only just check if a documented process is followed rather than see if the process has achieved its intention. Then management reviews where all the information on the above list is examined and the most significant problems are identified and action parties appointed to tackle them.

FINANCIAL BLACK HOLES   February 2019

12.1 Management Review

When data is presented at a management review managers congratulate themselves yet in too many instances they have no real information. This is illustrated by the fact that there is no drive to find out what is causing the problems or whether the problems have just been corrected or completely removed. (Corrective Action) That being the case, they cannot possibly make sensible decisions on what "Actions" should take place that would allow them to decide on opportunities for improvement. This is because they do not receive any meaningful date (information) at the management review.

To summarise; when Information is supplied it should allow management to make decisions on what needs to be done. Management need to appoint appropriate people with the relevant competence to achieve the task of eliminating the problem to ensure it does not reoccur.

There are many tools that can be used to achieve this, such as identifying the cost of the nonconformity (CONC) and using Pareto analyses to identify which problems are causing the most impact on the business to then implementing the improvement.

There are many quality Gurus such as Deming, Crosby, Juran etc who have put in place the processes and tools that can be used to help organisation improve.

Many organisations have a certain number of activities that have to be redone. Juran uses the term "Chronic Waste" to indicate where the same problem occurs over and over again. In many organisations, it becomes accepted as being normal with no effort being made to carry out "Corrective Action" which is where the organisation identifies why something has gone wrong (Root cause of the problem.) Then takes action to ensure it does not reoccur in future.

It is this failure to recognise that this waste of resources prevents organisations retaining their income. There is no point working hard to earn money and gain new business to find that, through your own failures, money is being wasted by having to carry out activities again.

FINANCIAL BLACK HOLES   February 2019

The approach of the Quality Guru Deming and his PLAN, DO, CHECK, ACT (PDCA) is now clearly identified in the introduction to ISO 9001:2015.

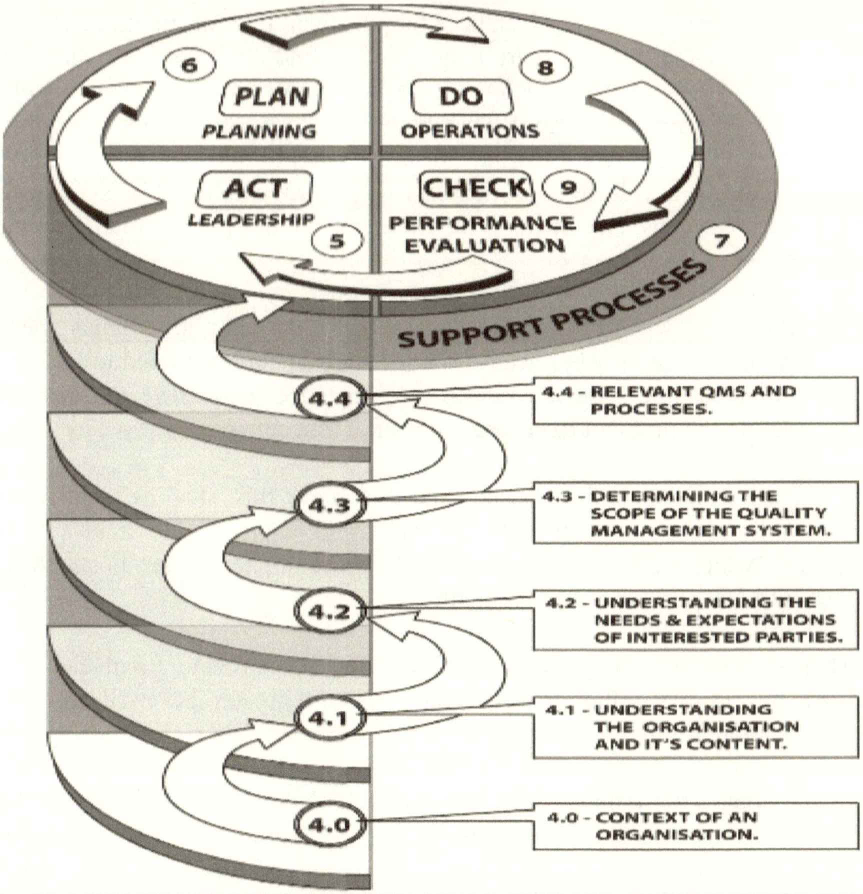

©2015 PDQMS

This shows the structure of the PDCA cycle with the ISO 9001:2015 clauses included.

(PDCA) is described as follows: -

Plan: establish the objectives and the processes necessary to deliver results in accordance with customer requirements and the organisations policies. (CAN YOU DO IT?)

Do: implement the processes.
(DO WHAT YOU PLANNED TO DO)

82

FINANCIAL BLACK HOLES   February 2019

CHECK: monitor and measure processes and product against policies, objectives and requirements for the product and report the results.
(GATHER THE INFORMATION ON HOW WELL THE PLAN HAS WORKED)

ACT: take action to continually improve the process.
(USE THIS INFORMATION TO DECIDE WHAT NEEDS TO BE IMPROVED AND ALLOCATE RESOURCES TO IMPROVE THE PROCESSES)

The diagram also shows how the clauses in section 4 need to be dealt with as they pass up to the organisations leadership for approval.

Not all organisations use the Plan, Do, Check, Act approach yet when you look at how it can be used to benefit the business it makes sense to implement it.

All organisations have to apply the "Plan and Do" approach and ISO 9001 covers this quite effectively, as it encourages a clear understanding of what the customer wants and asks the organisation to be sure they have the resources and skills to be able to achieve that requirement. Within ISO 9001 is also asks them to plan how it will be carried out.

Where smaller organisations miss out is they don't gather information about the problems they have experienced. In fact they see it as being of no interest once the problem has been **corrected** they just move onto the next job. This misses out on the opportunity to take **corrective action** where the cause of the problem is identified and effort made to prevent it happening again. Corrective action is intended to prevent money being wasted by stopping the problem happening again. In fact in many cases it is this waste that reduces the profitability of the business.

It is worth mentioning the misunderstood terms used in ISO 9001.

From **ISO 9000:2015** they are: -

<u>Correction 3.12.3</u>
Action to eliminate a detected non conformity
This is where you just correct what has gone wrong. It can be as simple as providing the customer with a replacement product that does meet the specified requirement.

83

FINANCIAL BLACK HOLES   February 2019

Corrective Action 3.12.2 (ISO 9000:2015)

Action to eliminate the cause of a nonconformity and prevent recurrence

Note: - As can be seen the revision above has restricted the Corrective Action to covering just a Non Conformity where the previous version covered any undesirable situation

Corrective Action (ISO 9000:2005)

Action to eliminate the causes of a detected nonconformity or other undesirable potential situation

This takes the issue further than **correction,** by investigating why the problem occurred, then taking action to ensure it does not happen again.

Preventative Action 3.12.1 (ISO 9000:2015)

Action to eliminate the cause of a potential nonconformity or other potential undesirable situation

This is used to ask organisations not to wait until things cause a problem but to encourage everyone to report anything they believe that could lead to a problem.

Note: - ISO 9001:2008 required a procedure for this ISO 9001:2015 does not.

These three terms are not always understood.

Correction is simple in that you just correct the error and that is allowed in ISO 9001. However it also requires you to carry out **Corrective Action** which means finding out the cause of the problem and doing something to stop it happening again.

Where the biggest confusion occurs is with **Preventative Action,** as too many quality professionals do not understand that if a problem has already occurred, then although you are being asked to prevent it occurring again that is NOT the meaning of **Preventive Action** as defined in ISO 9001.

This is quite clear if you actually read the definitions in ISO 9000.

Preventive action uses the term **"potential"** twice. **Corrective Action** states **"detected".** In other words if some nonconformity has already been detected it is not covered by "Preventive Action". Preventive Action is only applicable **BEFORE** a problem has occurred.

FINANCIAL BLACK HOLES   February 2019

This is quite clear if you recognise the importance of the Normative reference clause in ISO 9001:2015 where it states that ISO 9000:2015 is indispensable to the application of ISO 9001:2015. That is why I have on many occasions indicated that they are a **"Matched pair"** of standards. Even this statement is disputed by many quality professionals

As this book can be used by smaller to medium size businesses we will use a simple logical approach without complex methodology and terminology.

A technique I have used is the problem sheet. This is a simple A4 page similar to a Non Conformity Report that just captures information on problems (Attachment G).

To make the "Problem Sheet" stand out it is recommended that coloured A4 paper is used and the document is made readily available to all staff. An example of this sheet is Attachment E.

Literally it has a heading "Problem Sheet" location, problem number and the person who filled it in. The person who completes it can remain nameless if being anonymous helps get problem sheets completed.

It then has a space for the staff member or other to identify what the problem was,

Below the problem statement it has the Cost of Non-Conformance (CONC) and if possible what impact it had on the job. This can be manpower cost, new material used and any impact on the organisations credibility because of delay caused by the problem.

This "Problem Sheet" is just the front sheet of the document that gives an overview of the situation, it is then handed in to management or responsible party for further investigation.

This approach was used to capture defects over a specific Shut Down, where I was advised that no one would fill them in. It was written in English on one side and the local language on the other using the same format both sides.

During this 4 week shut down, over 100 Problem Sheets on light yellow paper were filled in. After analyses a direct loss of £250,000, plus an extra week added to the shutdown gave the information that could be dealt with.

85

FINANCIAL BLACK HOLES   February 2019

This waste was investigated and it was identified that ten of the problems caused a potential loss of £200,000.

This did not fit too well with the old 80/20 rule except regarding the costing however it met the principle of a small number of problems causing a large loss of both time and money.

Having this information allowed these issues to be prioritised using Pareto analyses and time was spent on Corrective Action on these 10 problem areas. These other problems were identified and some actioned, however the 10 problems were the priority.

This was just one improvement process which paid off as the next project was carried out on time and the losses were reduced to less than £ 75,000. (To those doing the math's new problems occurred) and benefited with a reduced time frame and smaller losses.

It was also identified that the most significant problem, that had caused the most loss, had occurred at least twice before and NO "Corrective Action" had taken place only "Correction".

These annual shut downs took place on a regular 5 year frequency covering the five similar units. (One shut down per year) In fact the time taken on each shut down was reduced because of this. Other changes that took place having gathered the "Meaningful Data" (INFORMATION) and having accurate information.

The first thing to do, as already stated, is to identify the problem

PROBLEMS

This leads us back to the beginning of problem solving.

It is essential that a problem statement is written. This can then be part of the Quality Objectives that are set for the organisation. It does of course need the problem to be identified hence the use of "Problem" sheets as they identify what the concern is.

So it is necessary to decide what an effective problem statement is, and what is not.

Problem statements should only define the problem

FINANCIAL BLACK HOLES   February 2019

PROBLEM STATEMENT
E.g. we have many instances where fitters are going out to the customer without all the equipment and tools they need to carry out the task. This causes many man-hours to be lost as they have to return to the workshop or retail outlets to obtain the material required.

A method of checking if the problem statement is good is to score it against the following four elements: -

- e) Is it a simple statement
- f) Are numbers (Figures) provided
- g) Is any background knowledge given
- h) Are any costs given

The scoring is simple and like any good system you score each element of the problem statement so if the problem statement is good it would score 10.

To keep it simple we can score each of the four elements at 2.5 marks each.
Note: - you can weigh the scoring if you wish. (Say 4 marks for cost)

This is a simple method to judge if the above "Problem Statement" is good.

REMEMBER THIS IS REALLY JUST A BEST GUESS
Using the KIS approach (Keep it simple) let us look at the problem statement

e) Is it a simple statement?
Yes it is simple and does give a picture of the problem
Score 2.0

f) Are numbers provided?
This could be the number of times this occurs and currently there are no numbers provided
Score 0

g) Is any background knowledge given
Yes it covers outside work however there may be other activities where this takes place
Score 1.5 or 2.0

FINANCIAL BLACK HOLES   February 2019

h) Are any costs given?
No there are no costs or information about how much this is costing
Score 0

TOTAL SCORE
4 out of 10 so it is not such a good problem statement

What other "Meaningful Data" would help?
You could mind map this and see what comes up. However for the purpose of the book, we will add the types of things that would improve the problem statement.

Point b) Are numbers provided? What would you like to see?
For example, over the last month there were 25 outside jobs carried out and 12 of them required people to leave the job site and spend time away gathering material

Seems useful, however which month are we talking about as that would make it objective. Would it be useful to also identify the number of man hours required to tackle the 25 outside jobs? What percentage of time is being lost? Hopefully you get the picture

Point d) Are any costs given? What would we like to see?
Assuming that the man-hours spent away from the workplace gathering material added up to 12 hours over the month in question. Seems useful but what percentage of the total man-hours for outside work does this cover?

Again good data but what is it actually costing in pounds? Should we use an average hourly cost of £35. Total cost £ 420. Should this be gathered over a few months?

Hopefully you can see what would help.

So let's rewrite the problem statement

FINANCIAL BLACK HOLES   February 2019

REVISED PROBLEM STATEMENT

We have many instances where fitters are going out to the customer without all the equipment and tools they need and carry out the task. This has caused 12 man-hours to be lost costing £420 in July alone as they have to return to the workshop or retail outlets to obtain the material. We therefore have had customers complaints about the delay and in some cases we have had to go back the following day.

This is not a perfect problem statement but it is a little bit better than before as it does give some level of information and would allow the problem to be investigated.

We still don't know if this is across just two crews of two people or twenty crews of two people. There is still a lot of information needed. It is however better than the first problem statement.

An interesting fact is no support will be given unless the costs are put in money terms.

In fact many quality managers use the "Cost of Non-Conformity" termed (CONC). As this can often make managers sit up when they see the cost in £'s (CONC.) It then gets a reaction. The downside is all organisations have what "Juran" calls Chronic Waste. This simply means waste that goes on and on forever as everyone ignores it. This is often where only "Correction" takes place not "Corrective Action" and is where the same problem reoccurs on a regular basis. This is often what is considered a small cost per incident but when it continues for years it adds up. That is why ISO 9001 is so keen on "Corrective Action" to remove this chronic waste. Even today many ISO 9001 Certified organisations only carry out "correction".

This is only a brief introduction and awareness of the benefits that could be obtained if the management system was set up to capture this information. Too many times people say they do not have the time to do this. This brings in the following statement

89

FINANCIAL BLACK HOLES   February 2019

I DON'T HAVE ENOUGH TIME TO DO THIS PROPERLY AS I AM TOO BUSY CORRECTING MISTAKES THAT HAVE BEEN MADE

As you can see, this is just a basic introduction but when your organization automatically gathers information on where time and money are being lost, it is not difficult to take action to remove these losses.

To all those quality professionals who may wish to ridicule this simplistic approach I will say it is aimed at any size businesses to help get then started, as many miss out improvement as they see it takes too long and is complicated.

Well it does not take a lot of time and it is not complicated.

In fact, it takes minutes to fill in a problem sheet and when they are evaluated over a period of time it can give sound objective information. It is not even necessary to take action over every problem found. All it does it allow you a choice. Simple common sense will let you decide if it is worth taking "corrective action". In some cases it will not, but you decide if it would benefit the business.

I would suggest you try it. I did this in a country where I was advised it would not work and I can assure you it did. Even if just one organization uses this approach, they will benefit by having information that they can work with to improve.

FINANCIAL BLACK HOLES   February 2019

13.0 - TRADITIONAL DOCUMENTED SYSTEM STRUCTURE

This section of the book is to remind readers of the basic management system that is used. It should be noted that a quality management system does not directly equate to a documented management system. In fact, the latest ISO 9001:2015 has removed any mention of required Procedures, or even the need for a Quality Manual, as the organisations Leadership should decide what is needed as in some cases only competent personnel may be required.

Traditional Documented Quality Structure

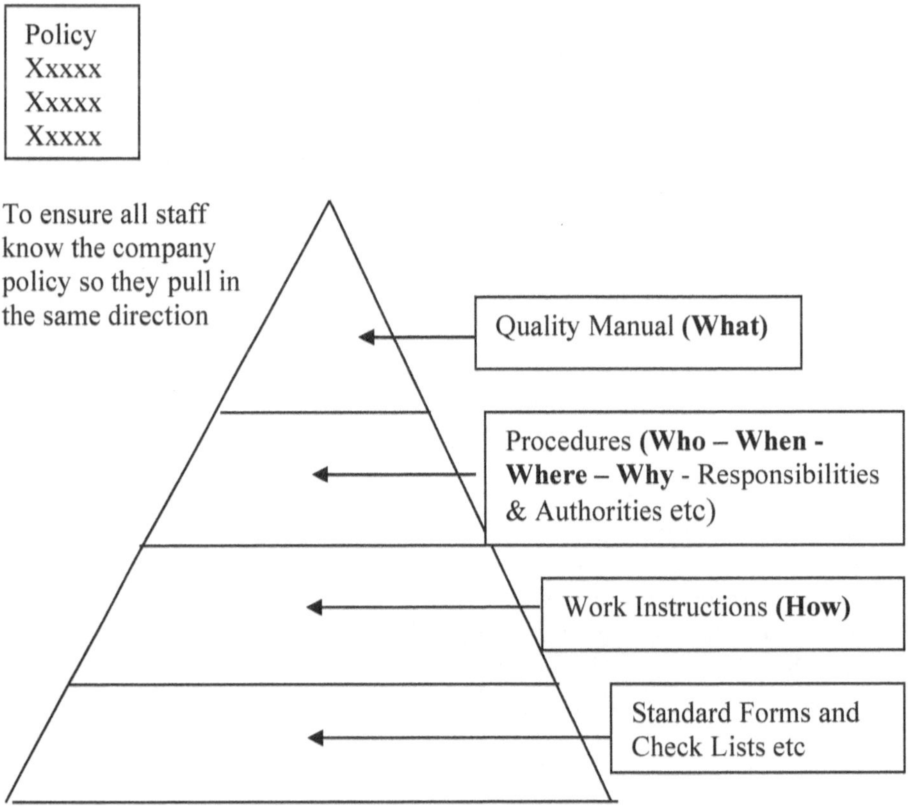

Policy
Xxxxx
Xxxxx
Xxxxx

To ensure all staff know the company policy so they pull in the same direction

Quality Manual **(What)**

Procedures **(Who – When - Where – Why** - Responsibilities & Authorities etc)

Work Instructions **(How)**

Standard Forms and Check Lists etc

FINANCIAL BLACK HOLES   February 2019

13.1 Quality Manual (WHAT)

Quality Manual (Clear statement by management regarding **what** the organization does)

This is the top level document, however it is no longer referenced in ISO9001:2015. It is however a very useful document as long as it is short and practical. It enables management to include the Policy and Objectives and explain what the organisation does. This information should be cascaded down to the personnel within the organisation as appropriate.

Some organisations put the Quality manual on their website.

There are practical reasons why it is a good idea to have a list of key procedures or documents within the Quality Manual. This is because they are useful for external readers to be able to cross refer to what the organisation does, therefore obtaining access to a list of relevant high level procedures. (This does not necessarily mean every procedure that exists just high level relevant documents).

The Quality Manual is often just seen as a manual to comply with ISO 9001. In many cases people do not understand its purpose. The document is to allow management to advise all personnel what their Policy, Objectives, Vision etc are. The document also clearly defines responsibilities and authorities for senior personnel, stating their position regarding these authorities and responsibilities throughout the company. Good companies sometimes combine all requirements including Quality, Environment and Health and Safety. Why have a Quality management system? The key reason is to structure the documents to meet the needs of the business. Companies with just one document have difficulty distributing the document to the right people. Having the right documents in the right place is part of the requirement for a Quality Management System. Large businesses may need four or five levels of documents with specific documents such as Quality Plans, Inspection and Test Plans. These are specific documents that when used effectively help companies run their business. All companies need systems, even small companies have systems for both their product or service and their administrative needs.

 FINANCIAL BLACK HOLES   February 2019

13.2 Quality Policy (HIGH LEVEL information regarding the organisations intensions)

It covers the overall intentions and direction of an organisation as expressed by top management.

This is one of the most powerful tools management have of getting a common understanding across to all staff. In many cases the Quality Policy is often provided to customers so they are able to see what the Organisations is all about.

It should be appropriate to the organisation and include a commitment to comply with specified requirements and improve the organisations management system

It will normally include a commitment to establish and review quality objectives

It is a requirement that all personnel should know and understand what the policy is. This is not word for word but in general.

It is necessary for the policy to be reviewed at appropriate stages to ensure it remains relevant.

13.3 Procedure (WHO, WHEN, WHERE, WHY)

Specified way to carry out an activity or a process. (Clause 3.4.5 ISO 9000:2015)

Procedures can be documented or not.

Procedures are a way in which you can break down activities into smaller documents so that they can be distributed to those that need them. They explain the Who, What, Where, When Why a task or activity is carried out. They are often broken down to departments and known as Departmental Procedures. The new standard ISO 9001:2015 continues to encourage companies to do things in processes. It is important to allow companies to decide how to develop their own structures that allow them to consistently meet their customer requirements and run their business effectively. It is also normally where leadership can clearly define each individuals responsibilities and authorities are made clear.

FINANCIAL BLACK HOLES   February 2019

13.4 Work Instructions (HOW IT IS ACTUALLY DONE)

These are working documents that allow trained personnel to carry out a task/activity in a consistent manner. They are usually quite simple and are for guidance. Very useful for shop floor or task specific activities.

13.5 Check Lists

These are a useful tool that lists specific tasks that require personnel to sign/mark/indicate if a specific activity has been done and whether it was acceptable. The big advantage of check lists is they can be maintained as a record. They also clearly identify regarding who checked or carried out each task. Provided they are realistic and at least initialed (Not just ticked) they are very useful tools and sometimes provided to customers to demonstrate what took place.

13.6 Standard Letters

These letters are often crucial to having a common approach to dealing with specific issues and therefore need too be controlled

13.7 Standard Forms

Most organisations use forms to capture information and to ensure all requirements are covered.

13.8 Drawings

A drawing is a fundamental methods of communicating requirements. They are always formally controlled. This method has been used for centuries to explain requirements. This method can be seen as being simple, however it does require the recipient to understand how to interpret a drawing. An example of poor understanding was when a drawing for a Knock out Pot for a refinery had clear orientation shown for the nozzles, yet the section view, used to show the height of the nozzles, showed all the nozzles in a line. The company making it missed the orientation drawing, therefore put them all down either side of the vessel like perforations along a stamp.

Their response when advised this was wrong was "Can we get a concession?"

13.9 Document Control

This is a "Key" aspect of an auditor's role.

Auditors should always ensure that the correct information is available at the point of use. Personnel need to have all the information they need to do the job properly first time every time.

FINANCIAL BLACK HOLES   February 2019

The previous ISO 9001 standard required a procedure to explain how the documented Quality Management System is controlled. This is no longer specified as a requirement however I would always advise organisations to have a procedure for Document Control, Records, Non-Conforming Product, Corrective Action and Audits, as this will ensure that the process is controlled in a consistent manner. This will help the organisations staff do things in the same way and be useful from an Auditors point of view, as it is essential that auditors are familiar with how documents are controlled.

13.19 Quality Plans (ISO 10005 Guidelines for quality plans)
These are usually developed where a company has to provide a non standard or different (Bespoke product) for a customer. Where an Organisation has standard products within its production the system itself is the Quality Plan.

Where, because of customer requirements, changes are implemented to the normal way of working then procedures and controls may have to be introduced. It may even require the customers own procedures to be used. It then enables the Quality Plan to control and point out which of the Customers and the Organisations own procedures and Work instructions are to be used.

It may even require writing new procedures or Work Instructions to cover any thing not part of the normal controls within the Organisation

This is a common structure but you do not have to have all these levels or even the same terminology as your structure should be one that meets your business needs

This is one example where the ISO 10005 Quality Management Systems Guidelines for Quality Plans might be useful to organisations that are involved in projects and working with customer requirements not just making their own products.

More detail is in the structure of standards is in Annex B of ISO 9001:2015

95

FINANCIAL BLACK HOLES   February 2019

14.0 - CONCLUSION, CONCERN AND OPPORTUNITIES

14.1 Conclusions

What currently takes place is, in too many cases, ineffective. It is recognised that what has been highlighted in this book may not be accepted by some quality professionals, as it is not what they have been taught. I can only ask that the reader maintains an open mind and look at the issues from a common sense approach. Would the output from the processes involved achieve the required purpose? The contention in the book is that in too many instances they would not.

14.2 Concerns

As can be seen from what has been raised in the book, there are many issues where the author believes that what is carried out by quality professionals fails to provide an effective service.

1. How can a review take place that does not actually look at what is actually occurring? Is just looking through documentation able to indicate that a process is effective?
   a. The scope did not allow the person doing the review to look at any actual complaints to see how they were handled
   b. In fact the person doing the review could not even ensure that the organisation actually followed their system never mind see if the processes were effective.

2. How can an organisation refer to a guidance document yet when the decisions are made, they are unable to justify their decision?
   a. The increase in height above the stated acceptable height of 4 meters for privacy, clearly stated in the report as being acceptable for privacy, has been overruled with no justification?

3. How can an enquiry that is looking into how a refurbishment of a building was carried out increase the scope to include whether the Statutory and Regulatory requirements need to be modified?

 FINANCIAL BLACK HOLES   February 2019

    a.   The scope was extended beyond the need to see if the refurbishment of the high rise building had been carried out to meet the applicable Statutory and regulatory requirements valid at the time of the refurbishment?

    b.   YES, it is true that other investigation may be needed however the enquiry itself should have been restricted to the refurbishment of the Grenfell Tower. Had this activity been carried out against all legal requirements that were relevant at the time of the refurbishment? Other issues should only take place if the current regulations are identified as being inadequate.

4. How can organisations that have recognised that what they have done was not effective only just correct what has been done?

    a.   In too many cases they fail to identify why the problem has occurred. They do not seem to understand the need to take steps to prevent it happening again.

    b.   This illustrates how the same problems keep occurring and the Chronic Waste is not reduced and is, in many instances, more likely to increase.

5. How can the so called "System Audit" meet the intention and scope of ISO 9001 when the audit should be trying to see if the processes being used are effective?

    a.   Some auditors have been trained to believe that they cannot audit without a procedure. No wonder systems are bureaucratic.

    b.   Auditors have been advised that they do not need to know what the product or service is as they are only auditing the system?

6. How can management reviews be effectively managed if there is little or no information provided to the managers?

    a.   Information = Meaningful data

    b.   In too many cases, it seems as if carrying out a management review is the objective and it does not seem to matter if it achieves anything?

 FINANCIAL BLACK HOLES   February 2019

7. Why is it that in many cases the only objective is to have carried out audits and management reviews as that demonstrates that they complied with the standard?

   a. Auditing is to see if processes are effective. Management review is to gather all relevant information and decide what, if anything, needs to be improved.

There are so many ineffective practices taking place that demonstrate that what is happening in the name of quality, can when ineffective be seen to be "Chronic Waste".

This is because the management system fails to achieve its intention of giving both the organisation and the customer's confidence, they believe that the system can consistently provide products and services that meet the specified requirements.

As long as professionals believe that having a documented system will solve all of an organisations problems, things will never improve.

In fact many organisation hide behind their system so they cannot be held accountable.

14.3 Opportunities

The author is looking for facilitators and trainers and other like-minded individuals to become trainers covering the importance of Management systems, Process Audits, Removing Chronic Waste and ensuring that organisations carry out effective Management Reviews.

If anyone is interested in getting involved in improving what takes place under the banner of quality kindly contact the author via email.
daveseear@btinternet.com

To those who are interested and can demonstrate personal attributes and competence in process auditing and removing chronic waste they may be allowed to use the material developed by the Author. He intends to takes a back seat from attempting to improve the credibility of quality. The journey began December 2009 and will finish in December 2019.

 FINANCIAL BLACK HOLES   February 2019

Provided selected individual are able to demonstrate effective use of the course material they will be given the course material to run the courses themselves.

Kind Regards - David John Seear a person who cares about what we provide!

 FINANCIAL BLACK HOLES   February 2019

ATTACHMENT A

26TH ANNUAL WORLD CONFERENCE

PROFESSIONAL PROCESS AUDITING AND REVIEWS

5THApril 2018

Actual feedback from 20% of the attendees at conference. All delegates were asked if they had any views on the presentation and the people who did respond gave the following answers

Conference feedback

1. Would you accept that complaints are just one of many methods that can be used to give an organisation an opportunity to improve?
    - Yes, The voice of the customer
    - Yes Complaints should be thought of as feedback for improvement
    - Yes Absolutely

    All other responses just one word Yes!

2. Is it an effective review if the person carrying out the review is only allowed to use the documents given to them by the "Organisation" and not allowed to see if what actually takes place is effective?
    - No! The independence has been compromised
    - No! This would be considered "Checking the box"
    - No! That would not allow the evaluation of the process only the documentation
    - No! – you need to verify or validate effectiveness

    All other responses just one word No!

3. Would it make things clearer if the terms "Documentation Audit" (Desk top review), "System Audit" and "Process audit" were always included in the report to clarify what took place?

100

FINANCIAL BLACK HOLES   February 2019

- Possibly, however people define some of those terms differently than you might define them
- Yes however a definition of each statement should be included
- Yes with an explanation of each
- Absolutely
- I believe so – the better resolution of information the higher the quality of the information
  All other responses just one word Yes!

4. Where the intention is to see if a process is effective, should the person carrying out the review clearly define that it is a "Process Review"?
   - Yes with definition and explanation to the auditee
   - Yes along with a clear scope
   - Perhaps as long as everyone is working of the same vocabulary
     All other responses just one word Yes!

5. Should we, as professionals, try to ensure that there is justification for what takes place and that the system being used is transparent and effective?
   - Yes as professionals we should make the system transparent and effective
   - Yes there must be justification or else why conduct it? It may be corrective or confirmation
   - Yes transparency is vital it goes with integrity
   - Absolutely, without this the audit will most likely not be worth the time
   - Yes provided the auditors thoroughly understand an organisations processes. In other words, they also have technical knowledge and expertise
     All other responses just one word Yes!

6. Should there be a qualification of "Professional Process Auditor" rather than using a general term "auditor" covering all types of auditing activities?
   - This may be a useful practice to ensure that process auditors are qualified and trained appropriately
   - If the term "professional" means that the person has technical expertise for one or more processes then "Yes"!. Otherwise I do not see how it will make a real difference

101

FINANCIAL BLACK HOLES   February 2019

- For some auditors they may need a qualification "Professional process auditor"
- It would make things clearer
- Not sure on this one. I feel most people assume "Auditor" means what you call a professional auditor"
- This would clarify the scope of the audit from the auditors perspective
- Yes, I think auditor can include professional process auditor so they can be identified
  All other response just one word Yes!

FINANCIAL BLACK HOLES   February 2019

ATTACHMENT B

Meeting with David Rutley MP Friday 30th June 2017

CLARIFICATION BASED ON: -

The issues raised on Page 1, 2, 14 and 15 of the Times Friday 30th June 2017

1. Introduction

The article on today's front page of the Times supports the two page document that I sent in on the 28th June. The "b" text below highlights concerns based on the comments in that article. The content of the pages attached seems to support my contention that the processes being used by the council are not adequate and are open to abuse. The structure of my previous 2 A4 pages is used to explain the concerns raised following the publication in the Times newspaper.

2. Issues of concern

This item regarding responsibilities and relationships should be dealt with first and as this has not been investigated so it is not covered in this meeting.

2. Validate the bid evaluation process to ascertain how the approval process has been carried out on organisations that are on the councils bid list

    a. I have found, in the past, that there is little accurate information held by the organisations on their "Approved Contractors list" and much of what exists is out of date.

    b. If the article in the Times is correct it would indicate that there is something seriously wrong with the process. There is no way in which an appointed contractor would be asked to reduce the price. The whole point of a sealed bid is that the party selecting the contractor has all the information they require before they award the contract. If this is true other contractors would have a case for the Council failure to appoint the contractor on the basis that they have successfully met the requirements of the contract. (Not the Lowest Price?)

103

FINANCIAL BLACK HOLES   February 2019

3. What Statutory and Regulatory requirements are relevant to the work being carried out?

    a. This should be defined in the enquiry. It would not be a surprise to find that not all the relevant statutory and regulatory requirements are known or understood.

    b. This is still a major issue as it seems that the price of the cladding was the issue and not the ability of the cladding to meet the relevant specifications

4. The criteria that "Approved Contractors" should meet

    a. Organisation should define their processes for approving contractors. I have often seen contracts given to organisations that are nothing but a "Sales Office" and work is sub-contracted. Even Sub-Contractors sometimes sub work out increasing the risk.

    b. It is still the responsibility of the party that appoints the contractor to ensure that their bid meets all the requirements of the enquiry

5. What checks are made on the sub-contractors by the council prior to the bid evaluation?

    a. It is not unusual to pass the enquiry to contractors who although approved are not competent in the work being offered. It is important to ascertain whether the contractor is competent to manage **ALL** the activities that are necessary for the successful completion of the contract.

    b. It seems that they only appoint the Contractor and have no idea who else is being used and the level of their competence.

6. Is the party letting the contract aware of the number of sub-contractors being used by each contractor bidding for work? (Modified text from original)

    a. If an effective control over the contractor is to be exercised then the sub-contractors that the bidder intends to use should be known and sufficient information about those sub-contractors obtained to verify their competence.

FINANCIAL BLACK HOLES   February 2019

    b. The competence of the subcontractor does not seem to
        be considered to be relevant by the contractor or more
        importantly the Council,

7. What checks are made on the sub-contractor prior to accepting
    them for the work they will carry out? Who does this check and is
    this specified in the contract?

    a. The importance of understanding the role of the sub-
        contractors working on behalf of the contractor and
        what actual work they will be doing is critical.

    b. I suspect that this activity is not carried out as the
        Council possibly considers this to be the contractors
        responsibility not theirs,

8. **What information (Meaningful Data) the council has on each
    bidder?**

    a. **This is the most important piece of information as
        in too many instances contracts are let to the lowest
        bidder. It is important to see how the bids were
        evaluated and what information was used to judge
        their competence.**

    b. This needs to be fully understood as it seems price is
        the issue

9. How is the bid process carried out and who signs off and approves
    the successful contractor?

    a. This is again a fundamental requirement as those
        making this decision should have enough knowledge
        of the activity to be competent in making that
        judgement.

    b. From the article it seems that the council has put
        pressure on Artelia to reduce costs and it is unclear
        whether this is after the contract has already been
        given or before

3. Conclusion

3.1 I have used my previous format to explain how these concerns
should be dealt with because from what I have read the council
will do what many councils seem to do and that is spend an
inordinate amount of money on legal fees to protect themselves.
They fail to recognise that they are supposed to provide a
professional service to their customers not just defend their own
systems no matter how ineffective they are. They are, or should

 FINANCIAL BLACK HOLES   February 2019

be, civil servants not a law unto themselves and should welcome the opportunity to improve..

3.1 On page 15 of the Times dated 30th June indicates that the judge appointed to chair the enquiry into the disaster said he was doubtful that it would satisfy survivors. (on page 15)

I understand that this is because of the restrictive scope he has been given which seems, from his comment, designed to restrict his ability to get to the truth.

FINANCIAL BLACK HOLES   February 2019

ATTACHMENT C

CONSCIOUS COMPETENCE MODEL

In evaluating competence there is a recognised format used that is known as the "Conscious Competence Model". It is familiar to most human resources and quality professionals and sets out four stages which can be summarized as: -

1. **Unconscious incompetence**, where the individual is unaware that they lack the skills, experience and knowledge to work efficiently and effectively, either because nobody has told them what to do or the standards to which they work are inadequate, non-existent or your efforts are considered irrelevant. In this state, it is extremely difficult to improve, since the person doing the job neither recognises the need nor do so or they have no incentive or encouragement to do so.

2. **Conscious incompetence**, this is where the person doing the job becomes aware of their inability to perform effectively, either through self-realisation or, more typically, because they are told that you are not good enough. In this state you can choose to seek to learn and improve through training, assuming that your organisation is sufficiently enlightened to provide such help, or you can mask your incompetence out of fear that admitting your skills gap will lead to dismissal.

3. **Conscious competence**, where the individuals seek improvement opportunities, and their organisation has both the resources and knowledge that enable you to close

FINANCIAL BLACK HOLES   February 2019

the gap between what is expected and what you are capable of doing, you learn to competently perform to an agreed standard in a systematic fashion.

4. **Unconscious competence,** where working effectively and skilfully becomes second nature. This is where you a have the knowledge to consistently carry out the role in an effective manner. It is second nature to you and there are no issues with the work that is being carried out.

FINANCIAL BLACK HOLES   February 2019

ATTACHMENT D

International Organization
for Standardization

International Accreditation Forum

Date: 10 December 2009

ISO 9001 Auditing Practices Group
Guidance on:

Audit Trail

The following paper by David John Seear is adapted from an article in IRCA's **INform** journal (Issue No.24, December 2009,
http://www.irca.org/inform/issue24/Seear.html)

1. Introduction
There are numerous important elements to carrying out a professional audit. Some requirements, such as the need to audit the process, are defined in ISO 9000. There is, however, one element of auditing that is missing in the terms and definitions in ISO 9000 – the *audit trail*.

The failure to carry out a process audit following an audit trail is the single most important reason why audits are not effective.

2. What is an audit trail?
In the absence of a definition from ISO 9000, a standard dictionary definition for 'audit' and 'trail' arrives at the following:

A systematic approach to collecting evidence based on specific samples, that the output of a series of inter-related processes meets expected outcomes.

109

FINANCIAL BLACK HOLES   February 2019

But what does this mean in practice?

Although applied by some auditors, the use of an audit trail is by no means universally accepted. It is the failure to ensure all audits employ process audits following an audit trail that undermines their credibility. Auditors should understand the path of the process that they are auditing and perform the audit accordingly, ensuring that the requirements of the process are being met.

For example, as a matter of course auditors will visit the shop floor. This enables the auditor to see what is taking place and to identify the specific order numbers of jobs that are going through at that time. From this information it is easy to identify in the sales department the agreed specification for that product or service and select relevant samples to be chosen. This means the process can be checked to ensure that what takes place is controlled and will meet the required specification. From here, the audit trail is picked up and followed through.

Using the audit of a purchasing activity as an example, you need to identify what material or equipment has been purchased for your sample order. It is always important to understand what drives the process. In this case, it is normally the requisition, which defines what is wanted.

If the auditor does not understand the specification, then he or she cannot check if the process being followed meets the requirements of the requisition.

- what does the requisition require – does this comply with the agreed specification?
- how is the decision to purchase made?
- how is the specification decided? Is it adequate?
- who decides what is required and do they have the authority?
- who chooses the supplier and by what criteria?
- what is the process for bid evaluation?
- how is the specification advised to the supplier?
- are national or international standards used?
- what controls the process?
- are there any special packing delivery requirements?

These are just some of the issues that need to be addressed, many of which follow the clauses of ISO 9001.

FINANCIAL BLACK HOLES   February 2019

3. Correct samples

The starting point for the audit is to use the chosen samples and identify the process path and the controls that were applied. It is vital that the samples are linked and come from the same trail. Too frequently, audit samples are taken at different stages of the process and are not related or linked to the initial sample chosen, which means that an auditor is unable to verify that the process is working. He will only be able to check if that particular document is filled in correctly.

Procedures, forms, checklists and so on, all ensure that a process is managed and controlled effectively. It is essential that auditors take the time to understand what is required from the process they are auditing.

It is impossible for a second- or third-party auditor to carry out an audit of an organization if the auditor does not take the time to understand the specification of its product or service, including statutory and regulatory requirements. It is this professional approach to auditing that allows the auditor to identify any weaknesses in the process and decide if an organization is capable of meeting the specified requirements. The audit trail approach applies to any audit be it an internal, second- or third-party audit.

About the author

David John Seear C. Eng. (daveseear@btinternet.com) spent 12 years at sea, where he reached the position of Chief Engineer, followed by 20 years with Shell UK, where he was appointed as 'Head of Quality and Performance' for Shell UK Materials. He represented the UK on ISO /TC176 for 3 years, as well as representing the Confederation of British Industry on the UK's mirror committee to ISO/TC 176. He now runs PDQ Management Services.

For further information on the ISO 9001 Auditing Practices Group, please refer to the paper:

Introduction to the ISO 9001 Auditing Practices Group
Feedback from users will be used by the *ISO 9001 Auditing Practices Group* to determine whether additional guidance documents should be developed, or if these current ones should be revised.

FINANCIAL BLACK HOLES February 2019

The other ISO 9001 Auditing Practices Group papers and presentations may be downloaded from the web sites:

www.iaf.nu
www.iso.org/tc176/ISO9001AuditingPracticesGroup

<u>Disclaimer</u>

This paper has not been subject to an endorsement process by the International Organization for Standardization (ISO), ISO Technical Committee 176, or the International Accreditation Forum (IAF).

The information contained within it is available for educational and communication purposes. The *ISO 9001 Auditing Practices Group* does not take responsibility for any errors, omissions or other liabilities that may arise from the provision or subsequent use of such information.

 FINANCIAL BLACK HOLES   February 2019

ATTACHMENT E

PROBLEM SHEET
(Note this is the front sheet providing an overview)

There could be many other documents used during the process added to this file

Location of problem ....

Problem Number .(normally next consecutive number then the year) e.g 05/19 5th Problem in 2019

Name ....   Date ....

Problem Statement – To be completed by anyone

Cost of Non- conformance (CONC) – This is an estimate of what it has cost the organisation to deal with it

Manpower   Material   and, if possible, impact on credibility

This is a straight forward estimate based on time spent dealing with the problem and any material used

Signed ....

Investigation into the Root Cause/s of the problem

Action Party/parties

**Names   Estimated Time
frame**

CORRECTIVE ACTION PLANNED (To be completed by action party dealing with the issue)

Signed ....   Signed (Relevant manager) ....

To be completed by: (Date) .... Follow-up date ....

VERIFICATION (To be performed by independent party checking action taken to ensure problem resolved)

Corrective action complete and satisfactory ....Date ....

113

FINANCIAL BLACK HOLES   February 2019

ATTACHMENT F

Audit Plan
Company C
17th – 18th XXXX

NOTE Only the items highlighted in bold are the actual listed items in the Audit Plan
The text beneath is a simplified summary of what is carried out. This is to demonstrate how an Audit Trail may be followed. More detailed requirements follow later in this document.

Day 1

08.30 Arrival and walk around to review process
This arrival gives opportunity to review the process before the opening meeting. It also allows for any delay in arriving as the auditor can go straight to the Opening Meeting. The walk around allows current jobs to be identified and their Contract/Order Numbers to be noted. It also gives an idea of the layout of the Organisation.

09.00   Opening Meeting
No comment on this as auditors should all know the process for an Opening Meeting.

09.20   Quality Representative
This area is where the auditor can see how the Organisation manages its business.
-       **Review documented system (QM/Procedures/Standards docs etc)**
Where possible the Quality Manual, together with the Document Control Procedure will have already been read before arriving at the location. The issue status and controls can be discussed together with the register for these documents indicating their status.
-       **Review register of controlled documents (Inc National Int Standards etc)**
The controlled list of documents should be reviewed and controls and issues understood
-       **ISO 9001 Certificates and last report/any corrective actions**
Previous reports can be reviewed to ascertain if any issues have been raised and how well they have been closed out.

114

 FINANCIAL BLACK HOLES   February 2019

- **Previous Non Conformities/Internal Audits/Management Review**

The review of these documents can often tell the auditor how well management control the Organisations systems and how effective they are.

- **Customer Complaints/Customer Feedback**

Again it is important to see how these issues are dealt with and how much information there is.

- **Identify Process (Walk around if not already done)**

All the above can, in the first hour or so, indicate how well the Organisation manages its business. It indicates how good their Internal Audits are and how effective Management Reviews are. This is an opportunity to open discussion concerning the Contract Orders that have been identified and it allows questions to be asked about those specific orders. This can help decide which of the current vehicles should be audited.

10.20   Review what vehicles are in for service.
Check on what documents are passed down to the technicians working on the vehicles. Identify service schedule documents especially those related to the vehicles already chosen and are in for service.

- Identify any customers special requirements
- Finalise samples for audit

This is the opportunity to view the management system that is used to control this activity. To see how the vehicles are booked in and scheduled. Who does this is the information available for those taking orders adequate to ensure that the work can be done in the given time frame.

Obtain any documents that relate to the selected sample of jobs going through that day.

11.00   Planning
- **Review programme for chosen contracts/Purchase Orders**
- **Identify any special requirements**

Identify how the Organisation plans the work and identifies any unusual or special requirements. The system should be able to handle standard contracts easily.

11.45   Sales
- **Review customer requirements order number etc**
- **Identify requirements**
- **Review Marketing Documents/Sales Literature**

115

FINANCIAL BLACK HOLES   February 2019

This is where the detail of the actual specification for the service is chosen. It is where special or unusual requirements can be picked out. This is the start of the formal Audit Trail. It is where the auditor skills pick up on the unusual or critical requirements as well as some general requirements. This information, together with any applicable drawings, work instructions or procedures are identified. It is also gives the opportunity to see how effective their liaison with their customers is. Have they given the customer accurate information on what will be done and how much it will cost.

It is also important to ensure sales literature such as special pricing, discounts and what will be carried out is unambiguous.

12.30. Lunch

13.00   Servicing
- **Obtain and use specific check list for the different types of service that will be carried out**
- **Control of manufacturing standard service list**
- **Follow process through and check documents in use and controls**

This is where the actual servicing activity takes place it covers each vehicle and how this information is passed down to the technician doing the job.

It covers all the controls that the Organisation has put in place. It is the chance for the auditor to see what is actually done. It includes seeing the facilities and equipment utilised and the competence of the personnel. Any testing that may be carried out. Examine the records that are kept together with the "Service Cards" and how they are controlled and retained as a formal record of what was done. It gives a clear understanding of what parts were used. During this process critical items, can be identified and noted for checking within the purchasing department. Equipment used during testing is noted for checking their calibration status.

15.30. Handling and Controls
- **Identify key components and controls**
- **Any special requirements Tolerances etc**
- **Markings**

Within this servicing area specific interest is noted of the handling and controls that are in place. It should be born in mind that this is customer property and must be looked after carefully. This covers tolerances, special processes such as welding, electronic testing equipment, judging when an item is no longer suitable and needs to be renewed and getting customer agreement before carrying out unscheduled work. e.g. Brake Pads. How is extra work managed regarding the time needed to do the work.

FINANCIAL BLACK HOLES   February 2019

16.30.   Review Findings and Feed back

This is an opportunity to identify what has been found, both good and of concern. This allows confirmation by the guide. Any concerns identified during the audit would have been advised to the guide at that time but may need clarification.

17.15   Close for day one

Day 2

Note it is always good practice to go over the findings in detail overnight. To ensure all Audit Evidence is reviewed and highlight any further clarification that may be needed.

08.15   Arrival
General discussion. (Progress to date)

08.45.   Purchasing
       Identify key components and controls
-   **Review Approved Supplier List (ASL)**
-   **Identify Critical Suppliers**
-   **C of C required (See guidance Documents 10)**
-   **Review controls within Purchase Order.**
-   **Any special requirements Tolerances etc**

This is another critical area because if the basic raw materials have not been correctly specified and obtained it is impossible to carry out a service that would comply with the manufacturers warranty.

From the items seen in the service area various items will have been identified and the method of ensuring they do meet the required specification should be examined. Are only manufacturers parts the only parts that are allowed to be used. This includes making sure all special requirements regarding Material Specification, Testing, Certification and any special processes needing control are specified in the Purchase Order.

10.00   Goods Receiving and Stores
-   **Materials receipt**
-   **Storage and control (Any Special needs)**
-   **- Issue of items to production**
-   **- Control of stock (FIFO)**
-   **- Condition of stock**
-   **- Control and Marking of products before despatch**

117

 FINANCIAL BLACK HOLES   February 2019

This is where the purchased material is received and controlled. It is where the received material is held prior to use by the technicians and must be held in a manner that enables, where required, traceability can be ensured. FIFO first in first out could be a positive way of ensuring material is not kept on the shelf until it is unusable.

11.15. Review final completion process and return of vehicle to the customer.
- **Review procedures/instructions**
- **Review completed documents**
- **How any additional activities have been cleared with the client**
- **Is the vehicle clean and in good order**
- **Review hand over to customer**
- **What information is given to the customer and what documents are handed over to the customer indicating what was carried out.**

This is where the Auditor ensures the service has been carried out effectively and all activities have been recorded and passed to the customer prior to final payment and release.

12.00. Training records/Competencies
- Sample staff and see records, confirm competences

The important thing regarding following an audit trail is to check on personnel seen during the audit and verify that the records held on them as individuals ensures that they were capable of doing the jobs they were seen doing. Use selective sampling of activities seen.

12.30   Lunch

13.15. Review improvement situation statisticsDespatch
- Management Responsibility
- Control and Marking of products before despatch
- Responsibility for despatch

This is the area where the product is finally despatched. Who is responsible, is there a C of C or a D of C (See Guidance Notes Parts 9 and 10)

13.45   Documentation and Records
- Retention recall and condition

All Contract requirements must be met to ensure a satisfactory conclusion to the Contract. It could include sending the correct documents, certificates, operating information etc. How is this Despatch recorded how would a recall work if necessary.

FINANCIAL BLACK HOLES   February 2019

14.15   Revisit areas for clarification (If required)
Review Audit evidence and develop findings and prepare report

15.45   Closing Meeting
This is where the auditor has the opportunity to advise the Auditee of the Findings. It is normal for auditors to identify where processes are well controlled and report these good areas first. If auditing is seen to be beneficial then it has to be a balanced audit. Audits that only discuss the non- conformities and concerns are not professional audits.

16.15   Questions discussion

16.30   Close

 FINANCIAL BLACK HOLES February 2019

ATTACHMENT G

BACK TO BASICS GUIDANCE DOCUMENTS

The "Back to Basics" documents were developed over many years of practical experience in order to assist students on the IRCA Auditor Courses. They covered some of the most misunderstood areas of the auditing activities.

WARNING

The documents that follow are not in any special order and do not always have approved formal definitions where they do they are identified. It should be recognised that in running training courses it is important to explain how each of the terms below may be used.

Each of these "Back to Basics" documents are written as "Stand Alone" documents so there is some repetition within these documents.

As shown in the case of "Audit Trail" there is no definition and that is why it is only a suggested definition. Also D of C and C of C have different interpretation but are becoming used more often and may need a common ISO definition as even C of C has different wording depending on who is using it.

GUIDANCE DOCUMENTS

1. **Audit Trail**

2. **Objective Evidence**

3. **Specification**

4. **Audit Criteria**

5. **Selective Sample**

6. **Audit Findings**

7. **Audit Evidence**

8. **Competence**

 FINANCIAL BLACK HOLES   February 2019

9.   Declaration Of Conformity (D of C)

10.   Certificates of Compliance (C of C)

11.   Controlled Documents

12.   Certification

It is recognised that not all personnel may accept all the comments in each Guidance Note but hopefully it may start a discussion that will resolve any issue of concern.

e.g. Audit Trail

The author would be pleased to receive any constructive comments both positive and negative in order to improve these guidance notes.

FINANCIAL BLACK HOLES   February 2019

Part 1 Audit Trail

See Attachment D - ISO 9001 Auditing Practices Group

Audit trail is one of the most important aspects of Auditing. If an audit trail is not followed then most that can be checked is whether the individual documents looked at are correctly filled in.
Dictionary Definitions

Audit

An Examination by qualified persons of, accounts of a business, public office or **an undertaking.**

Normally related to Financial Activities but latterly used by Quality Practioner's to assess the ability of an Organisation to comply with specified requirements.

Trail
Part drawn behind or in the wake of a thing

Track left by thing that has been moved or been drawn over a surface.

Track, scent or **beaten path.**

If the above are linked together we have: -

Audit Trail
An examination, by a qualified person, of an activity

Following the path that has been left by the process.

Note: - This importance of this is still not recognised in the ISO 9001 2015 Fundamentals and Vocabulary. This is such a shame and is one reason why audits are not always effective.

So what does this mean?

Take a simple purchasing activity

How is the decision to purchase made? Who decides what is required and do they have the authority? How is this advised to the supplier? Who

FINANCIAL BLACK HOLES   February 2019

chooses the supplier and by what criteria? How is the specification decided? Is it adequate?

- It is essential that a sample is chosen (This is the starting point)
- Then use the sample/s to identify the process taken such as: -
  o What drove the process e.g. what controls the process, how are decisions made.
  o Who has the authority
  o Who decides quantities
  o Who decides specification
  o How is specification controlled

The most important thing is to ensure that the samples are LINKED that they are from the same TRAIL.

If the Auditor is following the trail of a HORSE there is no point ending up behind a DONKEY.
Note: - this was the first and the original document issued in 2006 after ISO 9000 2005 had been issued

 FINANCIAL BLACK HOLES   February 2019

Part 2 Objective Evidence

This is, together with "Audit Trail", one of the most important aspects for an Auditor to understand if they are to do professional audits.

From past experience it is not always easily understood.

ISO 9000: 2015 section **3.8.1 Objective Evidence** is: -
Data supporting the existence or verity (Truth) of something.

Why is it important?
If there is Objective Evidence there can be No Dispute over the findings.

What is "Objective Evidence"

First look at "**Audit Findings**". **Section 3.13.9** of ISO 9000: 2015 defines **Audit Findings** as: -
results of the evaluation of the collected **Audit Evidence (3.13.8)** against the **Audit Criteria (3.13.7).**

©2015 PDQMS

FINANCIAL BLACK HOLES   February 2019

Audit evidence can be: -
1) Factual statements such as form SF 203 is no longer used.
2) Visual evidence such as the 12mm washers were kept in the storage shelf for the 25 mm washers.
3) Documented Objective Evidence such as: -
-     Five Purchase Orders were reviewed No's 230, 252, 276, 301 and 303 and two purchase orders No's 301 and 303 were not signed by the senior Buyer as required by Procedure QP 27 paragraph 16.2.

The factual statement 1) above, where something is no longer used, cannot be verified by Objective Evidence because actual evidence doesn't exist. This would need to be agreed with the auditees if this factual evidence was to be used in the audit report.

Visual evidence 2) is **Objective Evidence** as in the example above the location of the washers e.g. Bin Number 21 should contain the 12mm washers yet the 12mm washers were in bin Number 29 which should, according to the stores log sheet, contain the 25mmm washers.
Note: - The Auditee would normally obtain the Auditee or Guides agreement with this finding.

Documented evidence may be **Objective Evidence** if the specific items seen are identified and documented within the findings. It should be noted that the two purchase orders mentioned in 3) above that are not signed by the Senior Buyer e.g. P.O. 301 and 303 are, when written in the Non Conformity, actual objective evidence.

This may sound a little confusing but **Objective Evidence** is where **"IF CHALLENGED"** the Auditor can easily go back to the specific item looked at because it is identified in the Non Conformity.

If it is not possible to go back to the specific item of concern it would NOT be "OBJECTIVE EVIDENCE".

e.g. Non Conformity
"Procedure QP 27 Rev 4 Para 16.2 requires all Purchase Orders to be signed by the Senior Buyer. Two of the five purchase orders seen were not signed by the senior buyer".

Looks good? Wrong!! This non-conformity has no Objective evidence because it has not included the P.O. Numbers 301 and 303.

FINANCIAL BLACK HOLES   February 2019

Part 3 Specification

The term **"Specification" (3.8.7)** is defined in ISO 9000 2015 as: -
Document (3.8.5) stating requirements (3.6.4).

It is impossible to carry out a Professional Audit if the auditor has not looked at the **document stating the requirements** for any process that may be audited.

Let's also look at **Audit (3.13.1)**
Systematic, independent and documented process (3.4.1) for obtaining objective evidence (3.8.3) and evaluating it objectively to determine the extent to which audit criteria (3.13.7) are fulfilled.

We will come to **audit criteria** later in the guidance documents however one audit criteria for ISO 9001 audits is, of course, the ISO 9001:2015 standard itself. There are people who believe they are there to Audit to see if "the system complies with ISO 9001 2015?"
However they forget then to look at the standard itself that clearly states within the Scope: -
1 Scope
This International Standard specifies requirements for a quality management system where an organisation a) needs to demonstrate its ability to consistently provide a product that meets customer and applicable regulatory requirements.

The purpose of the audit is to see if the Management System is able to control the process in a manner that can ensure the product or service can consistently be met. The method of doing this is by judging the process used against the clauses within the ISO 9001 standard to verify that the system can achieve this.

Which then leads us back to **specification.**
The document stating requirements is usually the Purchase order or contract received from their customer. It is sometimes difficult for new auditors to understand that the term purchase order is used both for Customers Purchase Orders and the Organisation own Purchase Orders used to obtain material from their suppliers. For simplicity, in this article, **we will refer to customer requirements as the "Contract".**

The simplest form of contract is when the Organisation is making a product to its own specification. The process then is to look at the

126

FINANCIAL BLACK HOLES February 2019

specification identifying any special requirements or standards that are called up and going through Section 8 of ISO 9001:2015 (Operation) to ensure all the specifications are being controlled throughout the process. The more difficult type of contract is where the Customer specifies what is required as this then brings in more interfaces over the product and what is required.

Both Contracts will take the form of checking National and International standards within the contract as well as any other specifications including drawings where applicable. As the sample has already been chosen only requirements that relate to that particular product or service are examined.

This is part of the sampling process.
A professional auditor will always be looking for some critical requirement. It may be a special material, tolerance or clearance or an unusual standard that is called up. From this sample he will have identified a number of specific materials that needs to be purchased and from this the controls that need to be in place to meet the specified requirements.

This in turn leads to the purchasing department, where the requisitions or standard buying descriptions can be examined within the Organisation, to again understand the specification and check that all requirements are covered in the Purchase Order to the supplier.

The process then continues to the receipt of the material and what checks, material certificates, certificates of conformity, declarations of conformity are required to verify the material is acceptable. It may even cover acceptance criteria.

It is not the intention in this guidance note to go through the whole meaning of the ISO 9001 standard, but to give an idea of what should take place re verifying that the process does demonstrate the ability to consistently provide a product that meets customer and applicable regulatory requirement. The audit would cover all relevant requirements

This failure to comply with ISO 9001 2015 0.1 Introduction and Annex A and B is why audits have, in some areas, lost their credibility in the market place because clauses are used out of context.

FINANCIAL BLACK HOLES   February 2019

Part 4 Audit Criteria

Dictionary Definition: -
"Criterion" (n) a standard of judging; a rule by which opinion may be judged.
Note: - Criteria (Plural)
Audit criteria is the standard/s and/or specification/s being audited against.

ISO 9000:2015 definition of Audit Criteria in section 3.13.7
Set of policies, **procedures (3.5.8)** or **requirements (3.6.4)** used as a reference against which audit evidence is compared.

The normal criteria used for quality auditing can be: -
- ISO 9001 2015
- The companies management system
  o This may be procedure/s specified by the person planning the audit
  o It may be the full system
  o It may be a particular process
- The effectiveness of the process. (Does it fulfil the purpose)
- Any other relevant standard/ legislation/requirement

Note 1: -

- The Audit Criteria should always be written down and given to the Auditor when given the audit. It should also cover the scope of the audit. The scope is important as this may and usually does restrict the Auditor to a specific process/ location/area.
- The criteria is what the audit is measured against.

Note 2: -

- Auditor would need to obtain permission to go outside the scope.
- The Auditor can only link the findings to the allowable criteria

If for example the Auditor found a Financial Irregularity it would not be included in the audit report unless it could be called up against the Criteria that has been given.

Health and Safety will however will always be raised but again not included in the report unless it can be raised against criteria already given.

# FINANCIAL BLACK HOLES February 2019

Health and Safety is the responsibility of **ALL** personnel and must by Law be reported.

Note: - comments after someone has broken their leg "Do you know that staircase has been wet all morning you would think someone would do something!! I just knew that someone would get injured"

Legally if someone heard a person say that they could in the UK be taken to court for not reporting it as required by the Health and Safety at work Act.

Professional Auditors will be observant about all issues that help the company.

The auditor would of course mention this but not document the findings as part of their audit report if it is outside the Scope and not within the Audit Criteria. The same would apply if the Auditor found something outside the scope of the audit this again would not form part of the report. It would, however be important for the Auditor to report other findings where legally obliged to. It would need an extension to the scope or a modification to the audit criteria to include the area of concern within the formal report.

 FINANCIAL BLACK HOLES   February 2019

Part 5 Selective Sample

The term "Random Sample" has regularly been used by Auditors.

It is often understood to mean where the auditor takes a sample completely at random.

This is considered to be incorrect when carrying out professional audits.

Another term currently being used is "Selective or Representative Sample" which can be interpreted as an "**Intelligent** selection of **relevant** samples".

So is mean by this: -
- Professional auditors will look at the process being audited. What does the company make or do.
- Secondly what is relevant to why the audit that is being carried out.
- Finally look at what a company has been making recently.

A good thing to do is try to do a walk around at the beginning of the audit to see what is currently taking place.

In the case of a product being made what is on the shop floor.

In the case of a service what is being actioned at present.

Take an example of a 2nd party audit. The auditor/s will look at what product or service their organisation wishes to purchase. This enables them to look for similar products that are or have been produced for another company. The auditors will then look at this sample and select a relevant Contract or Purchase Order.

One item is not a sample. So the auditor may take two or three of the above directly related jobs and then one or two others totally at random to see how robust their system is.

This mainly depends on the time allowed. A 2nd Party Audit particularly if it is a large contract may only have time to sample just one to three contracts and not necessarily go through the whole process for all of them.

Where it is a simple process the auditor may sample twenty or more.

130

FINANCIAL BLACK HOLES   February 2019

The sample chosen is, from the auditor's point of view, a way of checking that the process is working. In doing this, the auditor wants to feel comfortable that the sample taken will give confidence that the system is working effectively.

Whether the sample is three or twenty plus is a decision for the auditor.

Take an example of a Hospital. The Auditor looks at what is being purchased and takes a random sample of 5 things. They turn out to be Paper Clips, Plastic waste bags, A4 paper, Ink jet cartridges and Light Bulbs.

Is the audit going to add useful information regarding the primary process within the hospital? Is the audit adding value?

Please do not misunderstand, it is important to have general items within the audit however we are back to the original statement the selection should be **Intelligent** and **Relevant** and that the auditor should feel the sample chosen gives confidence that the system is working and will allow the organisation to produce products or services that meet the customer needs.

Audit evidence is the documented records seen or the information obtained which can be compared with the audit criteria.

 FINANCIAL BLACK HOLES   February 2019

Part 6 Audit Findings

ISO 9000: 2015 section 3.13.9 **Audit Findings**
Results of the evaluation of the collected **audit evidence (3.13.8)** against
the **audit criteria (3.13.7)**
The evidence is everything found during the audit.

Audit Evidence (3.13.8)
Records (3.8.10) statements of fact or other **information (3.8.2)** which are
relevant to the **Audit Criteria (3.13.7)** and verifiable
In simple terms everything found during the audit that is verifiable

The normal audit criteria used for auditing are: -
- ISO 9001 2015
- The companies own management system
    - This may be procedure/s specified by the person planning the audit
    - It may be the full system
    - It may be a particular process
- The effectiveness of the process. (Does it fulfil the purpose)
- Any other relevant standard/legislation/requirement
- Any contract or order requirement

All or some of the above should be given to the auditor or agreed with the person responsible for the audit prior to carrying out the audit.

During the Audit, Audit Evidence such as "Factual Statements", "Visual evidence" where things are seen as well as "Documented Evidence" are gathered. All these things are noted on the report (Check List) that should contain both good and bad things that are found.

The Auditor uses these notes to decide what is correct and what is not. This is then compared with the audit criteria to see if it achieves and follows the specified requirements.

It is always important for the audit to be balanced with both the good findings as well as the bad. **Just reporting the bad findings is not good professional auditing**. In fact audits where only the bad things are reported often defeat the objective of helping the organisation improve as the Audit is seen as a negative activity.

132

FINANCIAL BLACK HOLES February 2019

During the audit the auditor will note many things. Not all these things will be reported. The Findings are the evaluation of what was found compared with the Audit Criteria. This enables the Auditor to produce the formal report, including Non Conformities and Observations that have been found.

Again professional audits **ALWAYS** report positives as well as negatives. The importance of this cannot be over emphasised.

If Audits are to be welcomed throughout the Organisation they must be balanced. In all auditing there are always good things to report. When both the positive findings together with the negatives are reported the audit becomes a welcome activity as it is seen to be fair and balanced.

FINANCIAL BLACK HOLES   February 2019

Part 7 Audit Evidence

Audit evidence is the physical objective evidence seen as well as the factual information obtained compared against the audit criteria.

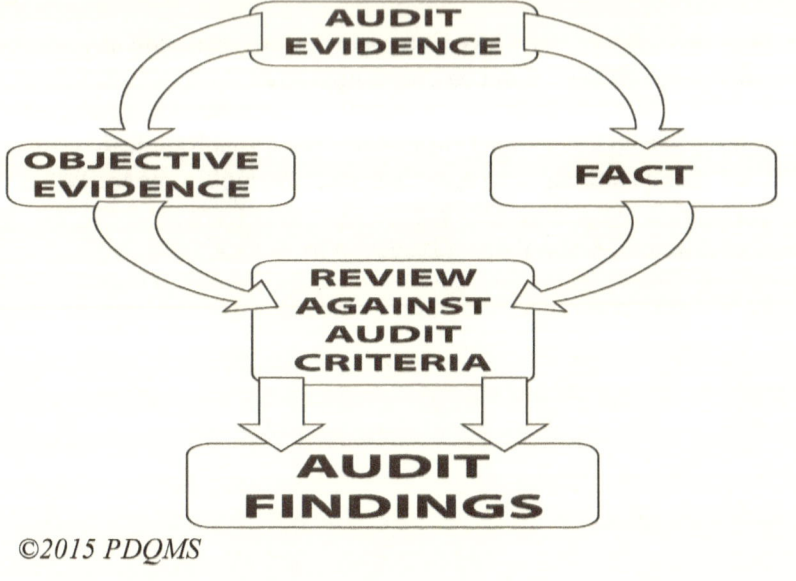

©2015 PDQMS

ISO 9000: 2015 section 3.13.8 Audit Evidence
Records (3.8.10) statements of fact or other **information (3.8.2) that,** are relevant to the **audit criteria (3.13.7)** and verifiable.

For example if a procedure stated that all Purchase Orders over £10,000 should be reviewed and signed off by the Purchasing Manager. Then during the audit the Auditor notices that out of the five Purchase Orders that were seen, only three orders over £ 10,000 had the signature of the Purchasing manager. The Senior Buyer who had produced these orders had signed the other two. The Auditor would then make a note of which orders were actually looked at. Then raise this against the audit criteria identifying the relevant procedure or the relevant ISO 9001 2015 clause as appropriate. The Purchase Order numbers of the two not signed by the Purchasing manager are the Objective Evidence. e.g P.O 13679, 14320 (Objective Evidence)

Audit evidence could also be where checking for a form that should be used it was found that it was no longer used. This is audit evidence in the

FINANCIAL BLACK HOLES   February 2019

way of fact but would not be Objective Evidence because it is not possible to go back and see that particular form as it does not exist.

It can also be where on checking the stock items all items were found in the correct locations and in good condition as well as being stored in a careful practical manner. The Auditor should always write down the items actually looked at. e.g The 2 inch cast Iron valves in box E23, The 0 – 50 bar pressure gauges in box F 19 and the 6" Ring Type Gaskets in box E 29 were all in the correct location etc..(This is good positive reporting as this was correct)

In simple terms the Audit Evidence is all the information both good and bad that has been recorded onto the Audit Checklist or Findings. It may be Objective Evidence or something that is missing and not seen or even something the Auditor was told about. Where the Auditor is verbally advised that something required by the procedure is not done he should check it by getting confirmation from those involved before recording it onto the Checklist.

Audit Evidence should cover both the **GOOD** things that are found as well as the things that do not comply or make sense.

It is from this Audit Evidence that the Auditor will develop the Audit Findings to be presented to the Auditee and their Management at the closing meeting. It is good audit practice to comment on the good things that are found. When the findings are reported the Auditor should be comfortable in reporting where processes were seen to be working well. E.g. If the stores area was seen to be well controlled this should be mentioned during the closing meeting. When this is done the auditee never normally asks to see the evidence of what was found however, the auditor should be able to, if requested, present the evidence that was found that allows the auditor to make that statement. It should never be "I think its good" or "it appears to be working well". It either was it was not. Always remember to advise the auditee that the audit only covers a sample and that this does not mean there are no problems anywhere else.

 FINANCIAL BLACK HOLES   February 2019

Part 8 Competence

Dictionary Definition: -
"Competence" (n)
Ability to do a task
"Competent" (adj)
Adequate, sufficient: properly or legally qualified
Competence
Properly qualified and with the ability to carry out a task correctly

ISO 9000:2015 Competence (3.10.4)
Ability to apply knowledge and skills to achieve intended results (New in 2015)

The judgement on how to ensure personnel are competent is crucial and at times can be a difficult task.
The first thing to decide and clearly define is what is required from the job that has to be done?
A job description is useful where it gives the description of the job and the capabilities required to achieve that. An example of a poor measure of competence is where the only judgement used is continuous repetition of the same activity without any evaluation of whether what was done was in fact done correctly.

An example of where to start is to define what needs to be done and what the required outcome is. This then leads to the skills and knowledge required. An example of how the Auditor can begin to identify competence is to ask personnel to confirm that they feel comfortable in doing the task assigned to them. Do they believe they have all the skills necessary to carry out the task correctly? This approach was tried many years ago with a surprising result. Equipment Inspectors who went to manufacturing plants to witness tests and inspections were asked to confirm their expertise in the areas they were being sent to work. To do this a list of generic products such as, Heat Exchangers, Vessels, Turbines, Diesel Engines, Valves, Pumps, Electric Motors etc were given to each inspector and they were asked to put: -

1. Knowledgeable
2. Satisfactory
3. Weak

This was done to ensure all personnel were comfortable with what they were being asked to do and to identify where there was limited knowledge and the skills profile could be improved.

136

FINANCIAL BLACK HOLES February 2019

It should be born in mind that all the inspectors were experienced and some with decades of work in inspection. The surprise came when one inspector who did most of the Pump inspection put a 3 (Three) down for pumps. On being questioned he admitted that when they did the tests and viewed the relevant charts e.g. NPSH he did not really understand what was going on and relied on the manufacturers staff to advise him if it was acceptable. He had also carried out pump inspection for another Organisation, as stated in his C.V., before joining the current Organisation. As can be seen experience did not make him competent. He was then sent on a training course at a pump manufacturers plant where he had not been acting as the inspector.

This highlights that repetition of doing a job is not a method of judging competence. In the instance above the only way this lack of knowledge would come out is when a pump failed to meet the specified requirements when it was in service and being used by the end user. This could have serious consequences.

The other problem area is where the understanding of what the task is supposed to achieve is wrong. If the organisation dealing with the competence issue does not know what is required then their method of judging competence will also be incorrect.
A classic example of this is the ISO 9001 Certification activity.

There are two schools of thought: -
1. ISO 9001 certification is about ensuring the Organisation being certified has a Quality Management System that complies with ISO 9001
2. ISO 9001 certification is about ensuring that the Organisation can meet customer, statutory and regulatory requirements relating to the product and the organisations own requirements.

This difference in requirement makes the judgment of Competence totally different for the two above requirements, as the knowledge required for one is different to the other.

The above only covers the understanding of what the auditor should be doing regarding the use of the ISO 9001 standard. The other competence requirement is, of course, a good understanding of the product or service being audited. Without this knowledge it is difficult for the auditor to add value and carry out an effective professional Audit.

 FINANCIAL BLACK HOLES   February 2019

There are Auditors who state they do not need to know the Product or Service as they are only auditing to see if the Management System complies with ISO 9001. As will be seen from this document this is incorrect. There is such a thing as a document review and this would be checking that the Management System covers the relevant requirements of the standard, however when actually auditing the Organisation the purpose is to ensure the Management System is capable of consistently meeting the specified requirements.

From above the view of the different Certification Body on how they measured Competence could be totally different dependent on which of the above schools of thought they accepted when judging Competence.

This could explain why the CQI has stated that Purchasing Organisations have reduced confidence in ISO 9001 Certification due to the significant variation in the Quality of Third Party Certification.

The truth is: -
ISO 9001 is a Tool not an Objective

FINANCIAL BLACK HOLES   February 2019

Part 9 Declaration of Conformity (D of C)

Dictionary Definition: -
"Declaration" (n) Stating and announcing, openly and explicitly, or formally; emphatic, solemn or legal assertion or proclamation.
"Conformity" (n) Compliance with
"Liable" (adj) legally bound answerable for

Declaration of Conformity n
A legal assertion that the item provided is in compliance with the specification.

The Declaration of Conformity is one of the common threads throughout the CE marking directives.

There is a need in certain industries to provide a Declaration of Conformity for every product that is made.

This is certainly true when Organisations provide equipment that is used in Explosive Atmospheres. (ATEX). The Declaration of Conformity may be used in many different industries where it is important to verify what the product complies with.

What does this mean?

In simple terms it is to ensure that each individual product produced has a certificate signed by a responsible person in the Organisation to confirm that the actual product they have provided does comply with the specifications called up.

What is the difference between this and the Order or Contract Requirements?

It is really to identify one individual within the supplying Organisation who is legally responsible for that product complying with the specification.

There is a misconception by senior personnel that when they sign this they are only signing to say the product is verified and validated to be able to meet its approved design requirements. Unfortunately this is not so. They are signing to say that particular product made that day has been made to the approved specification. They are therefore liable should this product,

 FINANCIAL BLACK HOLES   February 2019

for whatever reason, not meet the specified requirements in compliance with the approval given for that product.

When this is explained the first reaction is "Well I am not signing it as I don't actually make it myself". This is where a management system that is in compliance with ISO 9001 should, if applied correctly, give all the information necessary to ensure that each product does in fact comply. There are normally "Route Cards", "Check Lists", "Test Results", etc that if completed properly and traceable to the individual contract or batch number ensure that the product does comply. If the process for signing and issuing the D of C is only done when all the relevant activities within the process have been signed by the relevant Competent Personnel at each stage of the process, then, and only then, can a D of C be issued to go with the product. Obviously the person issuing the D of C must have checked that all the relevant documents have been completed and signed off by the competent personnel. The person issuing the D of C may or may not be the person who has signed the D of C. It is, however, the responsible party who verifies that all requirements have been met who is ultimately responsible but as long as each process has been signed off to be in compliance that should ensure that the responsibility is on each and every person in the process.

What should be in a Declaration of Conformity (D of C)

There should be the name and address of the Organisation that has made or put the product on the market. It should be noted that this Organisation is responsible for all issues relating to the Product and are responsible for ensuring any sub contracted activity is controlled as they cannot devolve themselves of the responsibility in any way whatsoever. It is their product and therefore their responsibility.

The D of C should then also contain the following for Atex Directive 94/9/EC: -

1. The name and identification mark and the address of the manufacturer or his authorised representative established within the Community
2. A description of the equipment, protective system, or device referred to in Article 1 (2)
3. All relevant provisions fulfilled by the equipment, protective, system, or device referred to in Article 1 (2).
4. Where appropriate, the name identification number and address of the notified body and the number of the EC-Type-examination certificate

 FINANCIAL BLACK HOLES   February 2019

5. Where appropriate reference to the harmonised standards.
6. Where appropriate, the standards and technical specifications which have been used
7. Where appropriate, references to other community Directives which have been applied
8. Identification of the signatory who has been empowered to enter into commitments on behalf of the manufacturer or his authorised representative established within the community.

Note: - it is impossible in a document like this to cover all requirements for all relevant bodies. Requirements can change and that is why it is important to be working with the latest Standards applicable to the Organisation.

E.G (Please note this is only an example and the relevant requirements should be checked)

For ATEX products Directive 94/9/EC requires.
Group II Cat 2GD Ex ed IIB T4
BASEEFA 1189 Buxton
Baseefa04ATEX1234 Latest Supplement Baseefa 04ATEX1234/3 13 Feb 2007
Baseefa 1180 Buxton UK
Harmonised Standard EN 60079-7:2003
Other Standards and Specifications: -
EN 60079-0:2004 (technically identical to EN 60079-0:2006 Harmonised
EN 50018:2000 (A review of EN 60079-1:2004 which is harmonised showed no significant changes relevant to this equipment.
EN 61241-0:2006 (State of the Art – intended for harmonisation)

This is just an example showing the type of information required to satisfy Directive 94/9/EC and the product approval requirements. These requirements can differ between regulatory bodies and it is important to check to ensure the relevant specified requirements are being met.

FINANCIAL BLACK HOLES   February 2019

Part 10 Certificate of Compliance (C of C)

Dictionary Definition: -
"Certificate" (n) Document formally attesting to the fulfilment of conditions.
"Compliance" (n) Action in accordance with request, demand
 "Conformity" (n) Compliance with

Certificate of Compliance/Conformity
Is a certificate that attests to the fulfilment of the specified requested requirement.

There is a need in certain industries to provide a Declaration of Conformity for every product that is made. (See Guidance Note Part 9)
There is however often a requirement for a certificate of conformity (Compliance) and this is often used for items that form part of a product.

If an Organisation requires material or machined parts to allow them to manufacture their product it is normal for them to ask for a Certificate of Conformity. (C of C).

The difference between a D of C and a C of C is that a D of C is normally what is required for a finished product where as a C of C is what is required for material bought in to make into a product. This of course varies with which country is involved and who is using the term.

The ministry of Defence has a **"C of C including traceability"**. Where it is defined as: -
A declaration by the supplier to the Acquirer that, apart from any identified and approved concessions the products conform to contract requirements.

It should be recognised that often the Product requiring a D of C may also be a part put into a final completed product however the difference is that it is, by itself, a complete and functioning product.

A C of C is often a requirement of the Purchase Order where it is a critical component or part of the final product. It does not of course stop the need for Material Certificates or Test Certificates that may be deemed necessary for confirmation that the item is to specification.

 FINANCIAL BLACK HOLES   February 2019

It may even need formal traceability as required by the Ministry of Defence.

Whether a D of C is more legally binding than a C of C is not in the Authors ability to comment on and advice from elsewhere may be appropriate.

FINANCIAL BLACK HOLES   February 2019

Part 11 Controlled Documents

What is meant by Controlled Documents?

There are two types of document in use in Quality management systems and they are "Controlled" and "Uncontrolled" Documents.

There can be a lot of confusion about what this means especially now that there are complete quality management systems all controlled on computer.

It is worth going back over the intention of having Controlled Documents when the system was just a "Hard Copy" paper system.

The ISO 9001 standard is quite specific in section 7.5.3 Control of Documented information is where it states controls needed to ensure that relevant versions of the applicable documents are available at point of use. This is quite easy to understand, as it is a sensible approach that allows personnel to work with the latest version of any documents. These documents are not just procedural documents but can be Drawings, Quality Plans, National and International Standards or any other document that is needed by the individual to do their job.

There have been many examples where if a copy is taken off the computer the copy is automatically identified as "Uncontrolled" only valid on day of print.

This approach is sometimes used as a method of ensuring that the system cannot be blamed if personnel use uncontrolled copies, however this is not the way to run a QMS. The QMS is supposed to work for the user not the user work for the system.

Going back to 7.5.3 above the intention of the standard is to ensure that the system controls the issue of the procedures and other QMS documents in a manner that all personnel have, at the point of use, access to the latest version of any documents they need to do their job. It is not acceptable to issue Uncontrolled Documents to personnel who need these documents on a day to day basis unless it is used that day: e.g. a check list that is filled in at that time. If it is a procedure then this should certainly be issue controlled to those without a computer.

This use of "Uncontrolled" documents is an area that is prone to error. If personnel have printed "Uncontrolled" QMS documents off the computer

144

FINANCIAL BLACK HOLES   February 2019

and use them because they need to refer to a Hard Copy version to do their job, then those copies should be hard copy "Controlled" documents. The suggestion that it is the users responsibility to check the issue status defeats the purpose of the QMS. The system is there to ensure that each individual has the latest versions in a format that enables them to do their work.

So what does Controlled documents mean?
In simple terms it means the individual issued with the document does not have to check the documents themselves to see if the version is the latest as the system will, when a new updated document is issued, ensure they are aware of or sent a new "Controlled" copy of the document. The holder may be asked to destroy or return the old copy dependent on what the procedure for Control of Document states.

This can, in a properly controlled computerised system, ensure that the holder has the latest version because provided there is access to the computer it will be the latest version. It is unacceptable for the system to demand that the user has to confirm whether they are working to the latest version, as the system should do this.

Uncontrolled Documents
Users of uncontrolled documents know they will not be advised of any revision.

There have been many instances where personnel who do not have a computer are issued with Uncontrolled copies. This is wrong and unacceptable as uncontrolled documents are documents issued for information only.

145

FINANCIAL BLACK HOLES   February 2019

Part 12 Certification

12.1 Why was ISO 9001 Certification Introduced?
The reason ISO 9001 certification was introduced was to reduce multiple assessments.

It started when one manufacturer, who was believed to be a Turbine manufacturer, stood up at a meeting called by the Government to improve the quality of British Manufacturing and explained that he could improve his efficiency if he was not audited by the buying organisations so often. On being questioned he explained that he had been audited over 40 times in one year. These audits consisted of teams of two to four personnel over two to five days. He also indicated that the Auditors were basically going over the same ground and it was this repetition that was galling.

He went on to say that he had four full time staff that did nothing but look after these auditors and it was not unusual to have two audits taking place at the same time. When this stoppage time was added together with time lost answering the auditor's questions it made a big impact on the Organisations efficiency.

12.2 Why were Purchasers carrying out Vendor Appraisal or Supplier Evaluations?
During this period, which coincided with a Major development of Offshore Fields in the U.K. sector, demand was high and it became imperative to have more information on Vendors/Suppliers. When the government introduced the Scheme, where Certification Bodies were able to be approved by an Accreditation body to carry out Audits, to ensure Organisations had Quality management Systems that enabled them to demonstrate that they could meet the specified requirements.

12.3 What are audits carried out by Certification Bodies supposed to achieve?
If the reply is "to See if the Organisations complies with the ISO 9001 2015" they are wrong!!

ISO 9001 2015 is a tool not an Objective. It is a tool for the Organisation to ensure that they have the system in place to ensure that they can consistently provide a product/service that meets the specified requirements. It is also the criteria used by the Auditors to measure whether the Organisations have the Management System Requirements, Leadership Responsibilities, Resources, Opreational controls Realisation

FINANCIAL BLACK HOLES   February 2019

and finally the Measurement, Analysis and Improvement in place.to enable the Organisation to demonstrate that they have a Management System that will consistently meet customer requirements by producing products/services that meet the specified requirements. It also encourages Organisations to actively look at improving the product/service as well as the processes being used.

ISO 9001 IS THE TOOL NOT THE OBJECTIVE

To do this effectively during an audit, Auditors must follow AN AUDIT TRAIL. (See Part 1 Audit Trail also IRCA Inform Audit Trail and ISO 9001 Auditing practices Group Att D)

FINALLY as a lot of personnel who carry out training tend to major on sections 4 to 10 of the ISO standard they forget to advise students what the general requirements ISO 9001 (Section 0.1 General) clearly states: -

This International Standard can be used by anybody to assess the organisations ability to **MEET customer statutory and regulatory requirements applicable to the PRODUCT** and the organisations own requirements.

Auditors should therefore concentrate on ensuring that the Organisation has the Management System and the statutory and regulatory requirements relating to the product in place to ensure it meets the PRODUCT specified requirements.

"THIS CAN ONLY BE DONE IF AN AUDIT TRAIL IS FOLLOWED"

 FINANCIAL BLACK HOLES   February 2019

REMINDER
ISO 9001 2015

Introduction 0.1 General Section
This International Standard indicates that the benefits to an organisation of implementing a quality management system based on ISO 9001 are the ability to consistently provide a product that meets customer and applicable regulatory requirements.

Note: - The statutory and regulatory requirements called up in ISO 9001 in the Scope General Section 1.1a) only relate to the statutory and regulatory requirements that are applicable to the product.

See Scope Note 1 In ISO 9001:2015 *where it states in this International Standard the terms product or service only apply to products and services intended for, or required by, a customer.*

FINANCIAL BLACK HOLES   February 2019

ABOUT THE AUTHOR

David John Seear C.Eng CMarEmg FIMarEST FCQI CQP

He is a Chartered Engineer with a First Class Combined Chief Engineers certificate. He served in the merchant navy at various ranks finishing as a Chief Engineer with Blue Star Line. He then joined Shell as an Inspection Engineer at Stanlow Refinery and was promoted to Southern Area Inspector working for Shell UK Materials Services based in Shell Mex House London. In this role, he carried out inspection of products manufactured for Shell. He was then promoted to manager of the department covering Field Inspection, Expediting and Quality appraisal.
In this period he represented Shell on various committees such as the EEMUA Engineering Equipment Materials Users Association (EEMUA) where he became the chair of the Quality Management Committee. He then became a member of the BSI's QMS 22 Committee covering quality. From this he was nominated to be a representative of the UK on the International Standards Organisations TC 176 Committee directly involved in the revision of the ISO quality standards. His final role in Shell was Quality Manager (UMAQ).

He left Shell and became Head of Supplies for Brunei Liquid Natural Gas (4 Years).

FINANCIAL BLACK HOLES   February 2019

He was appointed Middle East Regional manager for a Certification Body based in the United Arab Emirates. In this role he covered the UAE, India, Pakistan, Iran, Bahrain, Qatar, Jordan as well as other countries in the region. On returning to the UK he was voted onto the Chartered Quality Institutes Advisory Committee (AC) by CQI members. He finished his 3 year tenure on the Advisory Council and stood down in September 2018.

He is currently a partner in PDQ Management Services www.pdqms.co.uk where he runs IRCA approved Training courses on behalf of a Certification Body and teaches Professional Process Audits. He does not support "Tick Box" system audits where auditors just audit the documented system. This approach often fails to audit the processes to see if they are effective. (This in itself is a Chronic Waste of time and money)

He has had many articles published and this is the 5th book, see progression of books following.

 FINANCIAL BLACK HOLES   February 2019

PROGRESSION OF BOOKS

Each of the books were developed in an attempt to ensure personnel trained in quality had a full understanding of the benefit that can be achieved when applying quality in an effective manner.

2010 - ISO 9001 Audit Trail was developed following an article published in the International Register of Certified Auditors (IRCA) INform journal (Issue No 24 10th December 2009). At the same time it was also published by the ISO 9001 Auditing Practices Group (APG) See Attachment D in this book. One of the Certification Bodies asked the author to explain what Audit Trail meant and that led to the 1st edition of ISO 9001 Audit Trail being published in March 2010. The contention being that the so called "System Audit" was in many cases unable to demonstrate that ISO 9001 Certification would be able to determine if the organisation could consistently achieve the customer requirements. That is why what should take place is a process audit following an audit trail.

2012 - ISO 9000 Family of Standards was published in 2012 at the same time as the revision to ISO 9001 Audit Trail. It was published because auditor training did not always mention that **ISO 9000 was indispensable to the application of ISO 9001.** This failure of the training organisations to cover the ISO 9001 Introduction and clauses 1 - 3 meant that the requirement clauses 4 -8 were, and still are, misused as delegates were unaware that ISO 9001 was just one of the ISO 9000 Family of Standards. In the new ISO 9001:2015 the 3 standards ISO 9000, 9001 and 9004 are now called the "Core" standards.

2014 - ISO 9001 Back to the Future was developed from the draft DIS/ISO 9001 where there were errors. In the back of the book 10 of these were identified and this information was passed to TC/176 by the author and many of these were addressed before the issue of ISO 9001:2015.

2015 - ISO 9001 Into the Future was written to highlight the importance of reading all of the standard and not just clauses 4 -10 as just referring to these means the clauses will be used out of context. This required reading the Introduction as well as Annex A and B because failure to do so would mean the standard could not be used in an effective manner. Some definitions were modified within ISO 9000 2015 and the changes were illogical. This has been picked up again in the latest book Financial Black Holes

FINANCIAL BLACK HOLES   February 2019

2019 - How to plug financial black holes was developed after it was identified that many activities that were supposedly able to judge if a process was effective are, from a common sense approach, untenable. There are daily examples identified in any newspaper or news broadcast. The book was to be called How to **avoid** financial black holes but following investigation it was seen that it is too late to avoid Financial Waste as it is already with us. Therefore in many cases, audits, reviews and even enquiries are part of Chronic Waste. It was difficult to choose which examples to provide in the book however each of the examples gives a different incite to what is happening

Conclusion

Unless some senior quality professionals look at the content of the books from a logical point of view, nothing will change. Currently what happens is often unproductive. The hope is that there are people who would welcome the opportunity to improve what takes place under the banner of quality.

As can be seen from the book covers, it has been a journey along a woodland **Trail** to a **Pond**, then a **Windmill** before it reaches a **Satellite** finishing in a **"Black Hole".** All the books have been an attempt to improve training and understanding of the ISO 9000 Family of Standards" (Now termed "Core" standards) to ensure the activities that take place provide information and are beneficial.

Email daveseear@btinternet.com

FINANCIAL BLACK HOLES

February 2019

PROGRESSION OF BOOKS BY DAVID JOHN SEEAR FROM 2010 TO 2019

ISO 9001 AUDIT TRAIL ISSUE 1 2010 ISO 9001 AUDIT TRAIL ISSUE 2 2012

ISO 9000 FAMILY OF STANDARDS 2012

ISO 9001 BACK TO THE FUTURE 2014

ISO 9001 INTO THE FUTURE 2015

HOW TO PLUG FINANCIAL BLACK HOLES

www.ingramcontent.com/pod-product-compliance
Lightning Source LLC
Chambersburg PA
CBHW031415210526
45464CB00005B/1893